CONVICTED

The first time sent him to prison.
The second time set him free.

MELANIE SCHERENCEL BOCKMANN

REVIEW AND HERALD® PUBLISHING ASSOCIATION
Since 1861 | www.reviewandherald.com

Published by Review and Herald® Publishing Association, Hagerstown, MD 21741-1119

Review and Herald® titles may be purchased in bulk for educational, business, fund-raising, or sales promotional use. For information, e-mail specialMarkets@reviewandherald.com.

The Review and Herald® Publishing Association publishes biblically based materials for spiritual, physical, and mental growth and Christian discipleship.

The author assumes full responsibility for the accuracy of all facts and quotations as cited in this book.

Texts credited to NKJV are from the New King James Version. Copyright © 1979, 1980, 1982 by Thomas Nelson, Inc. Used by permission. All rights reserved.

Scripture quotations marked NLT are taken from the *Holy Bible*, New Living Translation, copyright © 1996. Used by permission of Tyndale House Publishers, Inc., Wheaton, Illinois 60189. All rights reserved.

This book was
Edited by Kalie Kelch
Copyedited by Rhonda J. Christiano
Cover design and illustration by Bryan Gray
Typeset: 11/13 Bembo

PRINTED IN U.S.A.

16 15 14 13 12   5 4 3 2 1

Library of Congress Cataloging-in-Publication Data
Bockmann, Melanie Scherencel, 1974-   .
  Convicted : the first time sent him to prison, the second time set him free / Melanie Bockmann.
      p. cm.
   1. Andrew. 2. Christian converts—United States—Biography. 3. Prisoners—United States—Religious life. I. Title.
   BV4935.A63A3 2012
   248.2'46092—dc23
   [B]
                                2011047561

ISBN 978-0-8280-2641-3

For Csyan

You may be bigger than I am,
but you'll always be my little brother.

Other books by Melanie Scherencel Bockmann:

In the Shadow of the Mob
Just Plane Crazy
UnRapped

To order, call **1–800–765–6955**.

Visit us at
www.reviewandherald.com
for information on other Review and Herald® products.

Acknowledgments

Andrew Michell literally made his life an open book to me and took the phrase "Can you hear me now?" to a new level during the hours we spent in different time zones trying to talk via an elusive Internet connection. Andrew, your dedication and transparency continue to inspire me. Thank you for allowing God to use you.

Andrew's mom, Kathleen Michell, spent time answering my questions, showing me photos and letters, and unselfishly allowing me to probe tender memories so I could write this book. I appreciate you, Kathy.

Frank O'Dell patiently answered my questions and provided valuable insight into the prison system and Andrew's story. Frank, it was an honor to meet you. I hope someday you'll have the opportunity to hear stories of all the other lives you've impacted.

My friend, Sheila Field, knows I can't resist a compelling story, which is why she invited me to her house for lunch and introduced me to Andrew. My jaw landed on her kitchen table and stayed there all afternoon while I listened to story after story of Andrew's experience of how God led him. Sheila, if it weren't for you and your sneaky ways, this book would not have been written. You are awesome.

I'd also like to thank Roger and Bev McKown for inviting me to participate in prison ministries, and everyone who voluntarily goes behind bars to cooperate with what God is doing there. You are amazing.

Writing a book is like simultaneously living in two different worlds. Thank you to my husband and kids for repeatedly reminding me what day it is, for reading every random paragraph I put in front of you, and for telling me to stop pacing the floor and go write. I sure love you guys.

Chapter 1

Andrew felt his stomach muscles tighten and wondered if he was going to throw up on the floorboard. He could tell from the lingering smells in the back of the squad car that he wouldn't be the first to lose it in there, and they'd all understand if he did. Today was the worst day of his entire 15 years of existence.

Andrew leaned his head up against the chilled window and let his breath fog up the glass. For once, the invitation to occupy the back seat of a police car didn't involve handcuffs pinching his wrists or a dreaded phone call to his parents from a police station. This time, however, was worse. Much worse. Andrew squeezed his eyes shut and tried not to think.

Inside the house the medical examiner team was preparing to strap his 13-year-old brother's body onto a gurney and wheel it outside, past his mother's rhododendron bushes, and into the open doors of the waiting ambulance.

His brother's *body*. Andrew shuddered. It was so strange to hear the police refer to Chris as a "body." What seemed even stranger was how they had escorted Andrew to a police car so he wouldn't have to see his brother zipped into a bag and extricated from his bedroom. As if anything could be more traumatic than what he'd already seen.

This can't be happening. Andrew licked his lips and tried to swallow the thick film coating the inside of his mouth, but his throat tightened, allowing only a small, dry cough. *Chris can't really be . . . gone.* If only he could rewind the events of the past few hours and push the pause button just before everything went so terribly wrong.

Through numb, bloodshot eyes, Andrew stared at the red and blue lights flashing in a chaotic nonrhythm from atop the emergency vehicles littering the yard. Stubby tailpipes exhaled long poisonous strands of exhaust into the crisp air. Police and other uniformed personnel went in and out of the house like ants on an anthill while Andrew's father stood on the grass in his slippers, an empty expression on his face.

Even now, Andrew could still hear his father's screams in his head. Awful, agonizing screams that had emerged from a dark place of horror and had jerked Andrew awake from a deep sleep. "Chris is dead!" his dad's muffled voice had cried out from the other room. "Chris is *dead*! Chris is *dead*!"

Andrew had thrown his covers off, crashed out of his bed, and run barefoot down the hallway in what seemed like slow motion. The wallpaper pattern had blurred past him as he'd run toward the sound of his father's voice. At the end of the hall Chris's bedroom door was slightly ajar, and light spilled from the crack. When Andrew had pushed the door open, the scene in front of him seemed as if it were a set from a horror film. Through the curtains the early-morning sun cast twisted light patterns across the floor. Chris's room was in perfect order, as usual. His clothes for the next day were neatly folded at the foot of his bed, and his bed hadn't been slept in. The only thing out of place was his brother's motionless body. Chris was slumped over—knees on the floor, hanging by his neck from the top railing of the bunk beds they had shared when they were little.

Andrew had stood frozen in disbelief. *This has to be a mistake. Chris is playing a trick on us. A horrible joke. He always takes things too far. Any minute now he is going to look up and grin, and everything will be all right. And then I'll wrestle him to the ground and teach him a lesson.*

But Chris hadn't moved. Waves of comprehension had begun to course through Andrew's mind, each more painful than the last, and shock had stung his pores. Chris was dead. Andrew had looked down at his father, whose eyes were wild with grief, and had felt the urge to run as fast and as far from this place as he could; but for once, his feet wouldn't move.

The windows of the squad car made random clicking sounds as the sun came up over the trees and warmed the cold metal and glass. Andrew viciously kicked the back of the seat in front of him as the scenes from that morning once again ran through his mind. Tears fell from his eyes, leaving dark spots on his sweatpants. "You're so stupid!" he said through gritted teeth. "So *stupid*, Chris! You didn't think this through, did you? You never think *anything* through! How are Dad and I supposed to tell Mom? Huh? 'Hi, Mom, hope you're enjoying your time with your friends in Arizona, and by the way, Chris killed himself!' "

Shortly after the police arrived, they had ruled it a suicide—an open-and-shut case. But Andrew didn't believe it. Chris was immature and impulsive sometimes, but he hadn't wanted to die. Andrew sobbed and punched the door with his fist until his knuckles were bloody and all the fire had drained out of him. Exhausted, he leaned against the vinyl seats and rubbed his scratchy, burning eyelids. A slow calm came over him, his body giving him respite from the pain. Gradually his breathing slowed, and he dozed off.

When Andrew awoke, he felt peaceful for a moment before he remembered the present pain of reality, which waited for him with a grisly embrace. It all came flooding back in a montage of images and sounds: Chris was gone. Nothing would ever be the same. Not that things were great before, but they had just taken an accelerated trip from bad to worse. Tears returned with a vengeance, and their salty residue made his face burn and itch.

When a shadow fell across the seat, Andrew looked up and wiped his cheek with the back of his hand. Standing next to the police car, his dad appeared as a defeated man, visibly aging with grief. Dark shadows on his face made him look gaunt as he motioned at Andrew through the window and opened the door. "They took him," he said. "He's gone. Come on, let's go back inside."

Andrew didn't want to go back into the house of horrors. Both of his brothers had died in that house. First John, and now Chris. His heart thudded against his chest as he dragged one foot after another toward the front door. Behind him he could hear the crunch of gravel under the tires of the last vehicle as it left their driveway. They were alone. Dark windows loomed above the flower beds, where leftover autumn leaves had turned to lightly frosted brown mush. Andrew gripped the black aluminum railing and slowly walked up the steps. Every fiber in his being resisted, but he followed his father into the dim entryway of the house.

It was December 30, 1994, and lights still blinked on and off on the Christmas tree in the living room. His mom had decorated it. She had wanted to make it one of those sentimental family events where everybody strings popcorn and sings Christmas carols or something, but nobody else had been interested. Chris had gone off with his friends, his dad had retreated to the basement to watch TV, and Andrew had had his own stuff going on.

Now he just wanted to yank the lights out of the wall and throw the tree outside. Christmas was over. He looked down at the carpet and stared at a few bits of wrapping paper his mom must have missed when she cleaned up after their gift exchange. His mind flashed back to the rare moment the four of them had shared in that same room just a few days before. A moment of playful celebration, and more important, no fighting.

"What is this?" Andrew asked, suspiciously shaking the package with his name on it.

Chris laughed. "You'll like it. I swear. I picked it out, didn't I, Mom?"

Mom nodded and smiled. "That's what he wanted to get you."

Andrew looked at both of them for a second, and then stripped off the wrapping paper. He slit the box open with scissors and dug through the foam peanuts. Soda. Candy bars. Chips. Popcorn. Cookies. "You got me junk food!" Andrew said, grinning and punching Chris in the shoulder.

Chris rolled on the carpet, laughing. "I told you you'd like it! That's all you ever eat!"

Andrew peeled off one of the candy bar wrappers and took a big bite of chocolate and caramel. "Mmmm, breakfast!"

Chris dug into the pile of presents under the tree, knocking against the branches and sending a shower of pine needles down on his head. "OK, who's next? Here's one to me, from Mom and Dad." Chris tore off the paper and stared at his gift. "No way! No way! This is the coat I wanted! This is awesome! Thank you!"

Andrew remembered that Chris's coat was still hanging in his room. He'd only worn it twice. Andrew blinked and realized he'd been staring at the wrapping paper bits for several minutes. His dad had walked into the room and was standing behind him. He tried to put his hand on Andrew's shoulder, but Andrew shrugged it off.

"You OK, son?" his dad asked.

"Fine."

"If you want to talk—"

"I don't," Andrew said.

"OK. Look, you don't have to talk about it right now if you don't want to. But if you decide that at some point you want to talk . . ." His dad hesitated. "It would be healthy for you, Andrew."

Andrew stiffened, resisting the words coming out of his father's mouth. Somebody needed to vacuum up those bits of paper and pine needles. It was time for all of the ornaments to go into their containers in the attic.

"I'm not sure what to do next," his dad continued. "I guess we should wait until your mom flies in tomorrow to tell her. I can't bear to think of telling her right before she has to travel home alone. It would just be too much . . ."

Andrew wondered what would happen if he lit the Christmas tree on fire. Nobody had watered it since before his mom had left. It would probably explode—a giant ball of flames fueled by sticky pitch and dry pine needles. It would be epic. Maybe it would burn the whole house down.

"Then when she gets here, we'll have to make funeral arrangements . . . and burial arrangements . . ." Andrew's dad broke down into sobs that shook his body, and he clamped his face in his hands. "Oh, Chris! No! Why?"

Andrew cringed. The sound of his father's grief was frightening and unnerving. His dad was never emotional. He always held it together. Until now. And now he was pathetic. Andrew could feel it swirling inside him again—the dark storm of anger. For reasons he couldn't explain, the sound of his father crying filled Andrew with rage. "Stop! Just stop!" Andrew yelled.

Andrew bolted from the living room and down the hall. He couldn't get to his bedroom fast enough. He slammed the door, leaned up against it, and banged the back of his head on the panel several times to drown out the sound of his father sobbing in the other room. Turning around, he saw the pile of junk food Chris had given him for Christmas on his nightstand. He stormed across the room and swept it all off onto the floor, and then threw himself down on the bed and punched his pillow into submission. A few minutes later he reached down and pulled the covers up over his entire body. Even the darkness under the covers could not shield him. He hated his life. He hated Chris. He hated his parents. And he hated himself.

Life is so meaningless, Andrew thought. *John is dead, and now Chris. What's the point? It's totally irrelevant. Everybody lives, everybody dies. That's it. And then we all end up in the same place. Six feet under. And the world just keeps turning.*

Andrew heard a scratching noise at the door. He sat up. It was Chris's cat, Charlie, pawing at the door and meowing loudly. Andrew turned over, put the pillow over his ears, and closed his eyes. The events of the past two weeks were piling into one big nightmare, and it was all crashing down on him, crushing him.

The day before Christmas break had started, he'd been expelled from yet another school. This time they had just made up some excuse so they could get rid of him. Three days ago his girlfriend had told him she thought she might be pregnant. Last night his brother had killed himself. And tomorrow morning his mom was coming home. The oppressive darkness paralyzed him. He didn't even feel like getting high.

Chapter 2

During the holiday season at Seattle–Tacoma International Airport, there's a giant ribbon-wrapped wreath that hangs from the balcony over the baggage claim area, and hundreds of poinsettias stand guard like red sentinels from every flight counter. Inevitably, coffee-fueled travelers swarm the common areas, coming back with sunburns and sombreros from Christmas in Mexico, or bundled in scarves and gloves preparing to say goodbye to relatives after a Northwest holiday.

Andrew slouched in a row of royal-blue faux leather seats and mindlessly watched the conveyor belt spit suitcases, car seats, and odd-shaped boxes onto the lethargic, revolving metal beast. Impatient travelers pushed and shoved each other trying to get a glimpse of their luggage, and then grunted as they wrestled suitcases and boxes onto the floor in an unscripted comedy of errors.

I hate people, Andrew thought. *It would be so easy to steal one of those precious suitcases and dump it somewhere before anyone even realizes it's gone. Now, that would be entertainment.*

Andrew's dad, along with some family friends who had come to be with them for support, sat talking a few rows away, waiting for the dreaded moment they would see Andrew's mom coming down the escalator and have to tell her the news about Chris. They didn't have to wait long. Her flight was on time, and the passengers from her plane were already disembarking.

His dad stood up. "There she is," he said.

Andrew stood and turned to look in the direction his father had pointed. When Andrew's mom saw him there with his dad, her face rounded into a bright smile, and she began walking toward them, but when she realized that other people had come with them, her smile gradually faded into a look of confusion and, finally, worry. She repositioned her purse strap on her shoulder and searched their faces. "What's wrong?" she asked. She looked from person to person, then at Andrew's dad with scared eyes. "Where's Chris?"

The drive home was unbearable.

Chris's funeral service was even worse. Chris's friends were scattered around the room in small groups, crying and hugging each other. Unlike Andrew, Chris had always thrived on social interaction. He had always made friends easily with his "Tom Cruise" good looks and gregarious personality. Also unlike Andrew, Chris had actually cared about what other people thought of him.

When the service ended, a stream of distant relatives and acquaintances made their way past Andrew and his parents in the reception line, each encounter with its own awkward hug and clumsy attempt at saying the right thing. It would have been easier if someone had told all those people that sometimes the right thing to say is nothing at all.

Andrew couldn't shake the feeling that he was on display: the only remaining son of Don and Kathy Michell, respected schoolteachers, friendly neighbors, and all-around good people. He could hear people whispering and see them looking in his direction.

"They seem like such nice folks," he heard someone say. "I just can't figure out what happened with their kids. It's horrendous."

"Well, with a suicide," someone else said, "it makes you wonder what's going on inside that home. I heard the other son has been kicked out of every school he's ever attended. Apparently he's a bright kid, but he's got a lot of problems. It's a good thing Don is retired. Keeping track of that one is probably a full-time job in itself."

Andrew felt a surge of anger in his chest. He wanted to punch something, and he might have if a heavyset woman that he'd never seen before hadn't grabbed his hands and squeezed them with her chubby fingers. "You poor thing," she said, wiping her tears on her shoulder. "Don't worry—everything is going to be fine."

Everything is going to be fine? Andrew stared at her as she continued talking, but he didn't hear anything else that came out of her mouth. *Is she kidding? My brother killed himself. How is everything supposed to be fine?*

A few minutes later a man came up to him and clamped his hand on Andrew's shoulder. "I know this is hard for you, son, but I want you to know that your brother is up in heaven right now looking down on you. God is taking care of him now. He wouldn't want you to be sad."

Andrew pulled away from the man's grip and pushed past the layers of people until he'd escaped into the fresh air outside. His head ached from crying and from the overpowering perfume of funeral flowers. He walked slowly, kicking at sprigs from some nearby fir trees that had shed their branches during the last windstorm. *These people are so bizarre,* he thought. *My brother is in heaven? How does that idiot know where my brother is? Or what my brother would or wouldn't want me to feel? He didn't know him. He was my own brother, and I barely knew him.*

"Andrew?"

Andrew looked up as his mom came around the corner. She looked exhausted. "There you are," she said. "We were looking all over for you. It's time. They've taken Chris to the burial site."

Andrew followed his parents across the expanse of manicured lawn to where people were already gathered. They lowered Chris's casket into the ground next to his older brother, John, at Fir Lane Memorial Park. Chris's grave marker was shiny and new and fit perfectly into a rectangle of fresh, black earth like the final piece of a puzzle. The bronze on John's grave marker had darkened with time and was framed by a cushion of green moss.

As Andrew stared at John's grave, he tried to think back to his death. Andrew had been 7 at the time, and Chris was 5. Although John had been older than Andrew by two years, he was a fragile little fellow with cerebral palsy. His brain had been damaged when he was born, the result of being trapped in the birth canal for too long without oxygen. He had never walked or talked, and had spent his entire life in a wheelchair. He had died of respiratory failure when he was 9. The way their mother had explained it, his little heart had just given out.

The graveside service was short, and Andrew was glad to go home. But even after the funeral, people came over to their house and lingered. Desperate for solitude, Andrew closed himself off in his room, put headphones on, and turned the music up as loud as his ears could stand it.

The door opened, and Andrew's mom came in with a plate of food. He slid his headphones off one ear. "What?"

"I brought you something to eat," she said. She stood there holding a plate that was piled with a sampling of all the food people had dropped off at their house during the past couple of days.

"I don't want it."

"Andrew, you need to eat something," her voice pleaded.

"I don't need to do anything," Andrew said. "I don't want it. Don't bother leaving it in here, either, because I'm not going to eat it."

He pulled the headphones back over his ears, lay back on his pillow, and closed his eyes. The loud music pulsed through his brain, mercifully purging out everything else. Music numbed him like a drug, like morphine in his veins. When he opened his eyes later, his mom was gone, but the plate of food was on his nightstand.

Before long the door opened again. Andrew pulled the headphones off and threw a pillow across the room. "Leave me alone!" he yelled. "Stop checking on me!"

The door pushed open further, and Lina poked her head in. "Seriously?"

Andrew relaxed. "Oh, it's you. Come in."

Lina closed the door behind her and looked around the messy room. "Like what you've done with the place," she said, absently massaging the back of her neck with her hand.

Andrew grinned at her attempt at humor, though he could tell she had been crying. Her black makeup puddled under her eyes, and her nose was red.

"Look," Lina said. "Sorry I didn't come talk to you at the funeral. It's just that there were all those people there and stuff. You looked busy."

"Don't worry about it."

"Would it be weird if I told you I want to see Chris's room?" Lina asked.

"No, of course not," Andrew said. "He was like your brother, too. Come on."

Andrew led Lina down the hallway to Chris's room. Charlie, who had claimed the top bunk and was napping, yawned and stretched his front paws when they walked into the room. Lina scratched behind Charlie's ears, then twisted her legs underneath her and sat down on the floor next to the green marker the police had painted on the carpet where they'd found Chris. Andrew sat across the room.

Lina picked up one of Chris's stuffed animals and hugged it to her chest. "I overheard Chris's girlfriend telling people that they had been talking on the phone and gotten into a fight the night he died."

Andrew snorted. "What? Is she trying to take credit for it or something? He didn't do it on purpose. I don't care what anybody says. He laid his clothes out for the next day. He was planning to be alive."

"Think he was just toying with the idea and went too far?" Lina asked, picking flakes of black polish off her fingernails.

"We've all done that. I twisted a coat hanger around my neck and hung it up in the closet once just to see what it felt like. Didn't actually want to die."

"Yeah, I know what you mean."

They sat there in comfortable silence. As close as they were, they'd never dated or made out. They were just really good friends.

"By the way, I found out that Ashlyn's not pregnant," Andrew said. "I think her friends talked her into testing me or something—told her to tell me she was pregnant to see if I really loved her. I guess I failed."

Lina shook her head. "I never liked her anyway. Too much drama."

"Yeah." Andrew stared at the shark poster on the wall. Chris had been fascinated with sharks. It figured that Chris would be infatuated with something dangerous. "I want to get out of here. I've got to get away from all this. Want to go to the store with me?"

Lina shook her head. "You know stealing's not my thing, Andrew. That's *your* thing. Besides, my mom will kill me if I get into any more trouble right now. I think my stepdad is getting sick of dealing with her problem child. They found my stash." Lina sighed. "That's $20 down the toilet."

"Tell your parents to stay out of your room," Andrew said.

"Yeah, like that's going to work. Look, I gotta go. If it's cool, I'll come by tomorrow, OK?" Lina gave Andrew a quick hug on her way out. "Take care," she said.

Andrew looked out the window at the setting sun. For such a gloomy winter, they had sure had a lot of sunny days.

Chapter 3

Andrew sat in the empty hallway next to a row of metal lockers. Buzzing fluorescent lights reflected off the glossy floors, and he could hear the janitor vacuuming nearby in one of the classrooms, drowning out the conversation between his parents and Mr. Shaw in the room behind him. He didn't need to hear the conversation. He'd heard plenty like it in the other schools he had attended. He had already known this was going to happen anyway. Showing up to Cedarcrest High School in the middle of the school year with a fat record had already put him on the administration's radar. He was a moving target.

Mr. Shaw, his valiant and overachieving algebra teacher, had made it his personal mission to transform Andrew into a model student. Andrew was inspired by the man's efforts—that is, inspired to introduce even more chaos into Mr. Shaw's little utopian classroom. Mr. Shaw obviously didn't know what he was up against, although a couple times Andrew had seen it flicker in his eyes during confrontation: Mr. Shaw was afraid of him too, just like his parents. Andrew rubbed his left shoe on the surface of the floor until he'd created a pattern of black scuff marks. *That should keep the janitor busy for a while,* he thought.

"Thank you, Mr. Shaw," Andrew's dad said as they came out of the classroom and shook hands. "I appreciate your time."

"You bet," Mr. Shaw said. "Nice to meet you both. See you in class tomorrow, Andrew."

"Maybe," Andrew said under his breath as he scooped up his backpack. He hated Mr. Shaw's nervous, condescending attitude and the way he pretended to be the epitome of educational professionalism in front of his parents. Tomorrow morning in class Andrew could expect him to be the same wilted piece of garbage that he usually was.

"Well, Mr. Shaw had a lot to say in our meeting just now," Andrew's mom said as they got into the truck.

"He always does," Andrew said. "You should try spending an hour a day in his class. He never shuts up."

"She meant about you, Andrew," his dad sighed, signaling and pulling into traffic. "Your behavior in class. He said you're a constant distraction to the other students, you damage school property, you interrupt the class—"

"He's lying," Andrew said, staring out the window.

"He also says he can't figure out how you're getting A's in his class when you never pay attention and you're always causing trouble," Andrew's mom added from the back seat.

"He's worthless!" Andrew retorted.

Andrew could see his father's grip tighten on the steering wheel. "Andrew, he's trying to help you. We're all trying to help you. Why would he say those things if they weren't true? My guess is he has enough to do in his overcrowded classroom without calling us into an after-school meeting to make this kind of stuff up."

Andrew dug his fingernails into the palm of his hand. He was going to cause so much trouble that Mr. Shaw was going to wish he had kept his mouth shut. Why couldn't everyone just leave him alone? He didn't need *help*. He needed everyone to just back off. He was sick of the meetings with teachers and principals, tired of the surprise "interventions" with family members and friends, and fed up with the parade of smug counselors who thought they knew him because they'd read a few books and had letters after their names.

Andrew could feel the familiar pressure of anger building inside him, and then snarling rage took over. He pulled his foot up and kicked it against the dashboard of the truck again and again until the glove compartment caved into a gaping hole. From the right door mirror Andrew saw his mother's terrified face in the back seat.

"Andrew, what are we going to do with you?" His mom's voice was the color of despair.

★★★

In the months following Chris's death, Andrew's dad spent more and more time in the basement at night, sitting in his stuffed chair watching TV. He was discreet about his drinking, but Andrew saw the glass recycle bin begin to pile up with wine bottles. Andrew's mom, if she was not at the elementary school teaching or grading papers and preparing assignments, spent most of her time reading books on grief or writing in her journal under dim lamplight.

Andrew hated being at home. Even on days when the wind chapped his knuckles and the cold rain numbed his face until he couldn't feel his lips, he would rather be outside riding his bike to a friend's house or to the mall than inside that stale sepulchre. Chris may have been gone, but his parents made sure his presence was still felt around the house. His room was still exactly the way he had left it. Andrew thought it was creepy, as though his parents were trying to preserve his space. As though they thought his brother might walk in at any moment and resume his life there.

They need to move on, Andrew thought. *It's over. He's gone.*

One day, before his mom got home from school, Andrew grabbed a bunch of Chris's stuff, made a pile in the backyard, doused it with lighter fluid, and torched it. Watching those things melt in the flames, Andrew felt strangely calm. His mom freaked out, though, when she got home. She got upset and raised her voice at him and cried; he yelled back at her. Andrew told her that Chris wasn't coming back and that she needed to let go. She told Andrew he didn't know what it was like to lose a son and asked him how he could do this to her. Andrew left on his bike and spent the night on a friend's couch.

The next day Andrew rode his bike home. He hadn't gone to school that day; he hadn't felt like it. He parked his bike in the driveway and went in the front door, shaking the rain off his jacket. His dad was standing in the entryway.

"Good. You're home," his dad said, car keys jingling in his hand. "We need to head into town. You have a doctor's appointment."

"What for?" Andrew asked.

"Your physical," his dad said.

Andrew sat in silence as they drove to town. He had been going to see Dr. Jay when he was sick and for regular checkups since he was a little kid, as had John and Chris. The familiar office looked the same as it had when he was a kid, including the posters on the wall and the well-worn stack of Dr. Seuss books on the little table, although the exam table didn't seem as tall as it had when he was little. When Dr. Jay walked in, closed the door, and sat down on his stool across from him, the atmosphere of the room suddenly intensified, and Andrew felt his blood slow to a crawl in his veins.

Dr. Jay leaned forward. "Andrew, I know you've been through a lot with your brother's death. Your dad explained to me that he's concerned because your behavior has gone from bad to worse. You haven't been listening, you've been causing trouble at school—"

Andrew felt his jaw tighten, and he interrupted Dr. Jay. "This isn't a physical, is it, Dad?"

Andrew's father remained silent.

"Dad?" he said through gritted teeth.

"Andrew, listen to me," Dr. Jay continued. "I'm going to prescribe a medication for you. A medication that will help."

"I'm not taking it," Andrew said. "I'm not taking anything."

Dr. Jay pulled his glasses off. "I'm your doctor, and this is your father, and you are going to do what we tell you to do."

Andrew bolted from his chair and tried to escape, but Dr. Jay was ready. He kicked the door closed with his foot. "No! Sit down!" he commanded. "You're going to sit down, and you're going to listen."

Andrew looked at the door, and then at Dr. Jay. *He was expecting me to do that,* Andrew thought.

Slowly Andrew sat back down in his chair. He sighed and carefully slouched down, bowing his head and folding his arms in defeat while he watched Dr. Jay out of the corner of his eye. After only a couple of minutes Andrew's posture began to have the exact effect he hoped for. Dr. Jay sat back on his stool, relaxed, and began talking about the medication he expected Andrew to take.

"Now, there are a few side effects, but nothing to be concerned about," Dr. Jay was saying. "When your body adjusts to it after a few weeks, many of the side effects will dissipate, and we'll start seeing some really positive results."

Andrew watched with stealthy glances until he saw Dr. Jay cross his legs and dangle one leather-shoed foot above the carpet. Andrew waited until Dr. Jay sat his clipboard down on his knees and began to write on the prescription pad, and then he made his move. He catapulted himself across the room before Dr. Jay could even get his legs uncrossed. He opened the door with enough force that it slammed into the doctor, and then he pushed past nurses and other patients as he stumbled through the stunned crowd in the waiting area.

"Stop him! He's crazy! My son is crazy! Someone call the police!" Andrew could hear his father yelling behind him, and that propelled him to run even faster.

Andrew shoved open the front doors of the clinic and ran across the parking lot into a wooded area near the freeway. The clinic disappeared from view behind him as he trudged through thick, wet ground cover and pushed his way through evergreen branches that bounced back and sprayed him with cold water droplets. Andrew knew two things: First, his father would never be able to catch him. Back pain from old Air Force injuries would prevent that. Second, nobody, *nobody* was going to reduce Andrew Michell to a medicated, drooling idiot, no matter how crazy they thought he was.

By the time Andrew came home that night, it had been dark for a couple of hours. It looked as though his mom had left some dinner out for him, but he went straight to his room. He had already eaten anyway. Several blocks ago he'd distracted the clerk at a gas station by pretending to flirt with her. She was giggling and twirling her hair around her thumb when he swiped the candy bars. He'd paid for one and stolen five. She had never known the difference.

He could hear voices from the TV in the basement, and he knew his father was sitting there alone, probably still trying to figure out what to do with his crazy son.

Am I crazy? Andrew wondered, looking into the mirror at his own reflection. *Maybe it's the other way around. Maybe I'm the sane one, and everybody else is crazy.* His cool blue eyes betrayed no reaction, even to himself.

Andrew lay down on his bed and kicked his shoes off. Part of him wanted to close his eyes and sleep after a long day, but he stared at the texture on the ceiling instead. His pillow was haunted with sweat from nightmares. He hadn't told anyone except Lina, but lately, closing his eyes in sleep locked him in an underworld of terror, with disturbing scenes of torture, suicide, cannibalism, and other nameless barbarities whose presence lingered even when he was awake. He reached over and pulled the dangling chain on his lamp so that light flooded the room. Maybe if he dozed off in the light, he'd be safe.

Chapter 4

In the living room there was a picture hanging on the wall. It had been there for years, and Andrew saw his mom look at it a lot. It was a blown-up snapshot of the five of them—Andrew and Chris were on their mom's lap, and their dad was holding John. They were all smiling. It was a Norman Rockwell moment that someone had captured with a camera, and it hung there in immortality.

That family didn't exist anymore, and to Andrew, no matter how his parents attempted to reframe the three remaining members of the Michell household, it would never feel like a family. But that apparently didn't stop his parents from trying.

Andrew could hear the soft sounds of his parents talking in the kitchen while his dad made dinner and his mom graded papers from her class. "Andrew, dinner's ready," his dad called.

Andrew came out of his room. "I'm going out."

Andrew's mom set aside her grading and began to toss the salad. "Andrew, please. Just come eat."

"I thought we could sit down and have a nice meal together as a family," his dad said. "Where are you going?"

"Nowhere," Andrew said, putting his jacket on. "Anywhere but here."

Andrew's dad stepped in front of him and blocked his pathway. "Andrew, what do we have to do to get through to you? Why are you doing this?"

"I'm leaving," Andrew said, trying to move past his dad toward the door.

"No, you're not," Andrew's dad said. "Not before you hear me out. Your mom and I have done everything we can for you, for all of our boys. We took you camping, we took you fishing, we took you to soccer practice, we took you to Boy Scouts, we even took you to that church camp; we have done everything we *possibly could* to give you a happy childhood. And this is how you repay us? And now Chris . . . and you . . ."

Andrew refused to let his dad's words penetrate. He was not going to listen to this. He looked at his mom. Her eyes were wet with tears. No, he wasn't going to let them drag him down into the abyss of their grief. Not tonight.

Before he realized what he was doing, Andrew snatched a pair of scissors from the end table. "I'll cut myself," he threatened. "I'll cut myself open right in front of you."

Andrew lifted up his shirt and let the point touch his bare skin. "You want to see me do it, or are you going to move and let me get away from this house?"

His mother's eyes widened at the sight of the scissors poised at Andrew's exposed abdomen, but his father's eyes hardened into resolve. "You won't do it," he guessed. "I've had it, Andrew. You're bluffing. Sit down and eat."

"You don't think I'll do it?" Andrew felt his lips curl into a smile.

With one swift move, Andrew stunned both his parents and himself. The scissors clattered to the floor, and his mother screamed. Andrew pushed past his father and ran out into the night, clutching his stomach.

It was 14 blocks to Lina's house, and by the time he got there blood had soaked through his shirt, and Andrew felt lightheaded.

"That's got to hurt," Lina said, cleaning his wound with hydrogen peroxide. She pulled waxy strips off the bandages and slowly positioned them on his abdomen. "At least you didn't go any deeper. You could have punctured something important. You know, like vital organs? Those things that keep you alive?"

Andrew sucked in air through his teeth and groaned as he looked down at his bandages. "I don't know what I was thinking. I mean, it happened so fast. I guess I just got so mad that I . . ."

Lina looked at him with an ironic half smile for a second, and then let her sleeves slide up her arms to expose her scarred wrists. "Really, Andrew? I'm pretty much the last person you need to explain anything to. I'm doing better now, but trust me. I get it."

A couple days later Andrew walked into the house and heard voices coming from the living room. He paused in the entryway, wondering if he should turn and leave before his parents ambushed him with another counseling session. Then he heard Lina's mom's voice, and he unzipped his jacket and walked in.

Lina's parents were sitting on the couch, and Andrew's mom and dad were sitting in the chairs. "Come on in, Andrew," his mom said.

"Is Lina here?" he asked, standing on the edge of the living room. On the wall above the couch the clock ticked loudly in the silence.

Lina's mom shook her head and put her hand on her husband's knee. "No, she didn't come this time. But we came because we want to talk to you."

"About what?" Andrew asked.

Lina's mom looked at his parents, and then began. "Well, when we first moved here from California, Lina was having a really hard time adjusting. Her father and I had divorced, I married her stepdad, and then we relocated here. She was really angry and withdrew from all of us."

"I already know all this stuff," Andrew said.

"But there's something you probably don't know," Lina's mom continued. "We were able to get Lina help. And that's what we've been talking to your parents about. There's a place up north, in Kirkland, where they have programs designed to help people work through their difficulties. It's a hospital that specializes in treatment for people your age. Lina went there. Did she tell you about it?"

Andrew shook his head. "Nope."

Lina's stepdad cleared his throat and sat forward on the couch. "Lina still has her issues. She's not perfect. But this program made a huge difference. We wanted you to know about it because maybe it could make a huge difference for you and what you're dealing with."

Andrew was silent. He hated counselors. But he *had* scared himself the other night with the scissors. He didn't realize he was capable of doing that kind of harm to himself, and each day since he'd had several painful reminders. He hadn't realized how often he used his stomach muscles until now. And changing the bandages on the raw wound was no picnic either. Maybe. Maybe if Lina had gone to this place, it might be all right.

"Why don't you just go up there and check it out?" Lina's mom suggested, partly to him and partly to his parents. "You can see what we're talking about. It's expensive, but it has really helped Lina."

There were a few moments of silence while the idea settled. To the surprise of everyone in the room, Andrew finally nodded. "All right," he said. "I'll check it out."

The next day Andrew sat in a chair and absorbed the opulent surroundings at the hospital while his parents talked with the doctors. He could almost breathe in the rich beauty of the decor. Lush red carpet covered the floors. The walls were a soothing pale yellow, decorated with landscape paintings and cherry wood trim.

He listened out of one ear while the director explained the program and his parents asked questions. Andrew began to breathe easier. This place didn't seem so bad. He'd felt tense about being admitted into a psychiatric hospital for treatment as an inpatient, but now he gradually relaxed as he listened to the doctor's calming words. "Specialized treatment program . . . unequaled in the country . . . finally get to the core of what he's experiencing . . . listen . . . compassionate . . . give him the help he needs . . . want him to feel comfortable . . . trust."

His parents signed the paperwork admitting Andrew to the hospital's treatment program, and then came the awkward moment of separation as a staff member came to lead Andrew away. His mom tried to hug him, but he shrugged her off his arm.

"I love you," she said anyway.

His parents stood with the director and watched as one of the staff members escorted Andrew toward the treatment wing. In front of him the doors unsealed and opened. Stretching out in front of him was a long sterile hallway with stark white walls.

Andrew stopped short. This was not what he'd expected. It looked like a scene from a psychological horror movie.

"This way, Andrew," the man said, smiling. It was the same fake smile that Andrew had noticed in the picture on the ID card clipped onto the man's shirt.

The lights flickered slightly, and Andrew felt the rhythm of his breath grow quicker as they walked through the doors and into the treatment wing. As they passed each open doorway, Andrew could see the expressionless faces of other teenagers who had been admitted into the program. Some were sitting at tables coloring on paper, while others hovered over a game of checkers in the corner. Others slumped in chairs staring out the window.

Their steps echoed on the glossy floors. Farther down the hallway, Andrew noticed an older teenage boy sitting on the floor with his back up against the wall. As he walked past, Andrew glanced down and recoiled at the sight of the deep scars stitched in crisscross patterns across his body, and the paper-white skin that stretched tight over his bony frame. The boy's unblinking eyes tracked Andrew's every move like a hungry jungle cat. "You don't want to *be* here," he sang in a mysterious sing-song. His eerie voice made goose bumps surface on Andrew's arms.

"I don't think I belong here," Andrew whispered to the staff member.

The staff member chuckled. "That's what everyone says the first day. Don't worry. You'll get used to it."

"What's going to happen to me?" Andrew asked.

"You'll go through an assessment," the man said casually. "Then we'll get your medication regimen started and determine what other treatment you need."

Andrew stopped suddenly. "No. I'm not taking medication. I don't need medication."

The staff member turned around. "Look, I don't care why you're here. But while you're here, you're going to do what we tell you to do, including taking your medication. If you won't take it willingly, we have other ways of administering it." He slowly simulated the movement of a syringe with his thumb and two fingers.

Andrew spun around. He could still see his parents' faces at the end of the hall. The doors were just starting to close, and Andrew made a run for it. "Wait!" he screamed. He pushed himself as hard as he could, his tennis shoes squeaking on the waxed floors as he bolted toward them. "Don't leave me here! Please don't leave me here! Don't do this to me!"

At the last moment Andrew lunged for the door, but it was too late. The doors heaved a sigh as they sealed closed in front of him, and he heard the lock shift into place. Andrew fell down on his knees. Other staff members suddenly came out of nowhere, wrestling Andrew to the ground while he kicked and screamed.

"You can't make me do anything!" Andrew yelled, twisting his body as their hands, elbows, and knees worked together to contain him. He fought as hard as he could, but the staff members finally crippled him with pressure points, and he fell to the floor with a moan.

"Oh, yes, we can," another staff member said through gritted teeth as they worked to pull his arms out behind him. "You're here, and you're going to do what we tell you to do."

They pushed him into a padded room and locked the door behind him. He was alone, trapped like a rat in a cage. He screamed until his throat was raw and he pounded on the door, but no one came.

Andrew sat on the floor and locked his knees inside his arms. He could trust no one, including his parents. He resolved that he would not cooperate—he would not sign anything, he wouldn't talk, and he wouldn't take their medication.

One thing he did know from listening to his parents' conversation with the doctor: because he had voluntarily admitted himself to the hospital, they could legally hold him for only 24 hours. Twenty-three hours and 47 minutes from now he was going to walk out of here. And the world was going to pay.

The hours passed, and the fire drained out of Andrew. He curled up in a ball on the floor. Later that evening Andrew heard the door unlock. A staff member opened the door and looked inside. "You ready to come out and play nice?" he asked.

Andrew wanted to punch him but instead he sullenly followed the man to a room with several beds. "This is your room. Those are your new roommates. Guys, meet Andrew."

Andrew lay down on the bed and looked at the blank white ceiling. Rage tempered only by resignation simmered inside him. The guys watched him for a while without saying anything, and then one of them slid forward to the edge of his bed.

"Hey," he said. "I'm Edward."

Andrew turned over so his back was to Edward. The mattress was hard, and the sheets smelled like bleach.

"What are you here for?" Edward asked. Andrew could feel Edward's eyes boring holes into his back.

Andrew didn't respond.

"Have it your way," Edward said. "Want to know why I'm here?"

"No."

"I'm suicidal," Edward said. "Four different times, I tried to kill myself by jumping off the Tacoma Narrows Bridge. Did you know it's 187-foot drop to the water? Should have died, but they pulled me out of the water alive four times."

No wonder he's locked up in this nuthouse, Andrew thought. *Now I know I don't belong here.*

Before the night was over, Andrew got into a fistfight with one of his roommates, a kid with strange eyes who seemed to think Andrew was sent by aliens to spy on him. It ended with a bloody nose and another swarm of staff members pulling them apart. The rest of the night Andrew lay awake, wondering if any of the other guys would try to attack him when he fell asleep. He could hear the screams of other patients echoing in the dim hallway, the intermittent shouts of staff members, and the creepy conversation one of the other guys was having with himself on the other side of the room.

Andrew felt suffocated by the hopelessness that seemed to creep through the ward and into each room. He could feel its humid, poisonous breath on his skin. It summoned fear from the deep place in his subconscious where his nightmares lived. It told him that what he feared the most was true: existence is meaningless. There's no purpose to life. The crazy people all around him were just walking dead waiting to take their last breath. And the end could arrive at any moment.

I'm going to do what makes me feel alive while I still have the chance, Andrew thought.

The night passed slowly and sleeplessly for Andrew. By the time the lights came on and breakfast was served the next morning, Andrew felt like a robot. A couple of hours later Andrew was sitting in one of the common areas trying to keep to himself when a staff member came to tell him that his parents had arrived.

This time the door buzzed open, and Andrew walked out of the treatment ward. His parents were waiting for him on the other side, and Andrew fixed his angry gaze on them. His muscles tensed with rage.

"Are you all right?" his mother asked.

"You left me here," Andrew snarled. "You heard me screaming. You saw me trying to get away. And you left me."

"Andrew, we didn't have a choice," his dad said. "We were concerned about you and thought this was the best thing for you. We love you."

"Well, I hate you. I hate both of you." Andrew looked at both of his parents to make sure his words met their target, and then he walked outside. As he watched the hospital disappear from view in the rear window of the truck, Andrew felt Category 5 rage brewing. It was only a matter of time before it would be unleashed.

Two days before school officially released for the year, Andrew deliberately walked out of Mr. Shaw's algebra class and pulled the fire alarm. That was his last day at Cedarcrest.

For Andrew, summer break started early.

Chapter 5

Andrew couldn't remember the first time he had stolen. He must have been about 9 or 10 years old. It was probably some candy or a toy he wanted. But what a rush! Before long, he needed that feeling like an addict needs a drug—that adrenaline rush that nothing else could give him.

It was always the same. It started with a restless craving that gnawed at his mind until he finally gave in. It didn't matter what he stole; as soon as he successfully lifted an item and walked away, the ravenous craving was satiated by perverse thrill. He didn't even need the majority of the things he took; he had money in his pocket to buy them. Sometimes he'd steal things, walk out, and throw them in the trash because he didn't even want what he had taken—he just needed the rush of stealing it.

Deep down he knew what it was doing to him, and to his friends and family. Some of his friends weren't allowed to hang out with him anymore. Nobody trusted him. If anything went missing, burned down, or was vandalized, he was always first on everyone's suspect list, whether he had actually done it or not.

Looking back, he vaguely remembered telling his mom, just before he had started ninth grade, that he didn't want to be a thief anymore. He didn't want to cause trouble or be the object of suspicion. He just wanted to focus on school, behave like everyone else, and be normal. Of course, that hadn't lasted very long. Two days into his ninth grade year some of his classmates told him that a teacher had left her laptop unattended in her classroom.

"You should take it," one of the kids had said. "Come on, you know you want to. It's just sitting there. They'll never know who did it."

Andrew had tried to resist the urge at first. But after the idea had been planted, it writhed inside him like a restless viper, and he couldn't think about anything else. He had finally sneaked into the classroom and shoved the laptop into his backpack. Ironically, the kid who had convinced him to do it was also the kid who turned him in later when the teacher discovered the laptop was missing. It was a setup, and Andrew again found himself sitting in the principal's office waiting for the police to arrive. The police had talked sternly to him and tried to scare some sense into him, but in the end they had left it up to the school and his parents to come up with an appropriate disciplinary measure. What a joke.

It's beyond my control, Andrew had thought. It was as though there was a force in his life compelling him to take, to vandalize, to destroy. So he decided that he might as well surrender to it. *It's part of me. It's part of what makes me who I am. I can't stop myself.*

That had been the moment Andrew had stopped fighting it. He was a thief. And there was nothing he or anyone else could do about it.

Since that day in ninth grade Andrew had begun to hone his craft. What was the point of being mediocre? If he was going to be a thief, he might as well be the best thief he could be. He began applying this rationale to other areas of his life. Likewise, if he was going to drink, he would drink himself unconscious. If he was going to get high, he was going to smoke until he couldn't get the joint to his mouth.

Andrew privately called the summer after his night in the psychiatric ward his "summer of crime." He watched the neighborhood happenings, studied his neighbors' schedules, and knew their weaknesses, as well as what valuables they owned. He discovered points of entry into their homes and knew how to escape without leaving fingerprints or other traceable evidence of who he was. He was amazed at how stupid people were. It was almost too easy.

Neighbors began reporting home break-ins, and the fire station was called to put out suspicious fires in the area, but they were never able to apprehend a suspect in the crimes. Crime was a game, and Andrew was winning.

Unbeknown to his parents and everyone else, Andrew began stockpiling stolen items of value in the house. His days were occupied with more daring and creative crime sprees, and parties and substances blurred his nights.

In the fall of 1995 Andrew began his sophomore year at Spanaway Lake High School. It wasn't long before he met a like-minded guy named Danny, and they became friends. Danny had connections with a formidable group of older guys at school—drug dealers who had a reputation for other criminal activities. Andrew was curious, but Danny wouldn't say much about them, other than that they were dangerous—not the kind of guys they wanted as friends. Rumors about the guys' alleged criminal activity surfaced and subsided, and it was hard to know what was true and what was simply legend. So Andrew resolved to find out for himself.

Some people would have been intimidated by them—the guys with sawed-off consciences who dealt drugs and flashed money and expensive jewelry at school—but not Andrew. He was tired of child's play. And if he handled it right, these older, experienced guys might be the ones to introduce him to the big time.

★★★

As usual, it took only three days for the bus driver to suspend Andrew from the bus for the rest of his sophomore year. Andrew was sure his picture had been posted somewhere in the school district bus barn, and all the bus drivers had been warned to watch out for him and kick him off the bus at the first sign of trouble.

The high school was farther away from home than his other schools had been, and Andrew detested riding his bike the entire way to and from school. He had managed to complete driver's education training over the summer, and since his sixteenth birthday was coming up in a couple of weeks, Andrew had an idea.

After riding his bike home from school in the miserable rain one day, Andrew decided to try to make a deal with his parents. A few years before, he and his mom had been in a car accident, and there was an insurance settlement that Andrew's parents had set aside for his college tuition. Andrew hoped he could convince his parents to use it for something else: a car.

"Absolutely not," his dad said, not giving the idea a chance even after Andrew had pleaded his case and presented his most compelling arguments.

"I'm sick of riding my bike to school," Andrew argued. "Look, it's raining outside, and I'm soaking wet. I'm getting my license in a couple of weeks. I need a car."

"I don't know, Andrew," his mom said. "I don't think it's a good idea. You haven't shown yourself to be very responsible. A car is a lot of responsibility."

With that statement Andrew lost his temper and pounded his fist on the kitchen counter. "I want a car. And I'm going to have one whether you like it or not. Either you can buy me a car or I'll steal one. Would you rather I steal one? It's up to you."

Andrew's parents looked at each other, and then back at Andrew. He could see they knew he wasn't kidding.

"That attitude right there is proof to me that you're not mature enough to handle the responsibility," his dad said.

Andrew was furious at his parents. "The money belongs to me anyway. It's my insurance settlement, and you set it aside for me to use for college. Well, now I want to use it for a car."

Andrew argued his case for several days. It took some time, but his parents eventually decided to give him the money they'd set aside from the settlement.

"I guess it technically belongs to you anyway, and your mom wants to give you a chance to prove yourself," his dad said, obviously still unconvinced they were doing the right thing. "Don't make us regret this decision."

Andrew searched *Auto Trader* until he found a car in his price range: a 1987 Ford Thunderbird. Days later he had a driver's license, a used car, and total freedom.

Much to his parents' pleasant surprise, Andrew got a job working at the fairgrounds. It was temporary, but it was a job.

Every September the fairgrounds in Puyallup, Washington, would come alive for 17 days. The Puyallup fair hosts more than 1 million visitors who come to stand in line for hot fresh scones dripping with raspberry preserves, a wonderland of thrill rides, blue-ribbon exhibits, and live animal shows, as well as rodeos and a star-studded lineup of concerts in an arena that seats an audience of 10,000. Andrew's job was to manage one of the game booths, selling tickets to people who paid for a chance to knock over milk bottles in hopes of winning a giant stuffed animal.

"They'll never knock them all over, though," Andrew's boss told him in a confidential hush. "Look, see? That one there's full of lead. It'll never fall down."

What a racket, Andrew thought. *People pay money to try and don't even know it's practically impossible.* "You guys must rake in the cash."

Andrew's boss laughed. "Like taking candy from a baby. All you've got to do is get them to come over here. If you can make their kids or girlfriends fall in love with one of the stuffed animals, guys will pay a small fortune trying to knock over those bottles."

By the end of the first day in the game booth, Andrew was bored out of his mind. The screaming from the roller coasters, the heavy smell of barbecue and roasted corn and cotton candy and manure, and the constant sound of baseballs hitting milk bottles gave him a headache. People waddled by stuffing their faces with giant, cinnamon-coated elephant ears or pushing their screaming kids in strollers, determined to have fun even if it made them miserable. He wondered why he had ever wanted this job in the first place.

Just then a tattooed guy with big muscles and a tank top walked up to the booth. Hanging on his arm, a girl in a halter top licked the edges of a giant blue swirl of cotton candy. Her eyes were dark with makeup, and she had piercings in all sorts of interesting places. "I'll take three shots at those milk bottles. My girl here has her heart set on that panda bear."

Well, good luck with that, pal. Andrew thought, taking his money and handing him the baseballs.

The first shot knocked over the top two bottles. Andrew put them back up. The second shot knocked over one bottle. The guy wound up for a third shot, aimed, and knocked over three bottles. The lead bottle was still standing.

The man cursed under his breath. "This is a setup, isn't it? There's no way to win?"

"Would you like to try again?" Andrew asked. "Five dollars gets you three more chances."

The girl smiled up at her boyfriend. "Babe, you can do it. You almost had it that last time."

The guy handed Andrew five more dollars. His next two tries were also unsuccessful.

"That's it," he said. "If I don't make this one, I'm done. Forget it."

"But I want the panda!" his girlfriend insisted. Pouting, she turned around.

At that moment Andrew thought of a way to make his dull job more interesting. "Hey," Andrew said in a whisper. "There actually is one way to win. You give me $10 under the table, and I'll knock the bottles over for you so you can have the panda. It'll be our secret. I'm happy, you're happy, and most important"—he motioned toward the girl—"she's happy. We all win. What do you say?"

The man looked around furtively and then slapped a $10 bill into Andrew's hand. Andrew stepped back as the guy threw his last ball at the stacked milk bottles. At the right moment, Andrew secretly tipped the fourth bottle. "Look at that!" he said. "We have a winner! Congratulations!"

"Thanks, man," the guy said in a low tone, nodding at Andrew over his shoulder as they turned and walked away with the prize.

Andrew grinned. In five seconds he had made more than his regular hourly wage. It was kind of genius, actually. Cheating the cheaters.

The next day Andrew tried out his new idea a few more times. His pocket was full of $10 bills when his boss came by the booth. "We've been having an awful lot of winners over here," he grumbled, examining the setup.

Andrew shrugged. "What can I say? Some of these people know how to play the game."

Andrew's boss looked at him. "Well, see if you can pull in some losers, OK? Remember what I told you."

Andrew waited a little while and let a few people lose. Toward the end of his shift he decided to try his own racket one more time. As soon as he'd taken the money and knocked over the bottles, however, two police officers appeared.

"You're under arrest," one of them said.

"For what?" Andrew tried to look surprised.

"Don't try to pretend you haven't been stealing. Your boss suspected you were taking money. We've been watching you. You're under arrest, young man."

A crowd gathered to watch as Andrew was led away from the fairgrounds in handcuffs. *You win some, you lose some,* Andrew thought. *Besides, I'm a minor. What can they really do to me?*

Chapter 6

Just as Andrew suspected, there wasn't much the police could do to him. After all, he was a minor, and stealing a few bucks from a game booth at the fair was not exactly grand larceny. After a single night in Remann Hall, the Pierce County juvenile detention center, Andrew was released to his parents and sent home.

October arrived. Fall moved into the Northwest with blustery winds that loosened the red and yellow leaves from the trees and twirled them in the air like puppets before discarding them on the ground. Gray clouds misted the blankets of displaced leaves with drizzle. The mood around the house grew more somber as the anniversary of Chris's death loomed only a couple of months away. Now that Andrew had a car, it was easier for him to get away. He spent most of his time getting high with his friends. When he was high, he could laugh his cares away and forget about reality.

Getting high was much better than drinking for numbing the pain. He had tried drinking, but he didn't like how out of control it made him feel, as if he were outside his body, watching himself do and say stupid things. He also hated the pounding dehydration headache that would wake him up the morning after and the way the world spun in circles around him and made him want to throw up.

As much as he had begun to hate drinking, he had started to enjoy smoking pot. He'd suck in the smoke and hold it in his lungs while a smooth, detached calm came over him. While he was high the anger went away, and everything was hilarious. He couldn't stop laughing at everyone, at everything. It felt so good to laugh for a change.

★★★

One day after school Andrew found Danny leaning up against his car in the parking lot. He was talking to another guy. "Hey, Andrew," Danny said. "Come on over here. I want you to meet someone."

Andrew walked over to his car and threw his backpack into the back seat.

"This is Dre," Danny said. "He's the one who gets me my . . . stuff. You know."

Andrew nodded at Dre. "Hey."

Dre nodded back, and then a moment of awkward silence hung between the three of them. "So," Andrew said. "Speaking of . . . stuff. You have any?"

"Not with me," Dre said. "I got some back at the house if you all want to come over."

Danny looked at Andrew. "I've got to head home. I'll catch you later."

"See ya," Andrew said to Danny. He looked back at Dre. "Sure. Hey, why don't you hop in? I'll give you a ride."

The two of them got into the car, and Dre gave him directions. Several blocks away Andrew pulled into the driveway of a house. When they got inside, Andrew recognized several of the guys who were there. It was the same group of guys Danny had warned him about.

Dre introduced Andrew to the group—Almand, Alan, Eugene. Andrew nodded at each of them, but they stared at him suspiciously. Andrew didn't blame them. Fortunately, after a few minutes and a couple of tokes, the guys warmed up to Andrew.

After that afternoon Andrew ran into them several different times—sometimes it was to buy drugs; other times they saw each other at parties. Over time Andrew could tell they'd begun to regard him as a like-minded individual and were less careful about their conversation in front of him.

"Is it true?" Andrew asked casually one night when they were hanging out together at the same party. "You guys are doing dirt?"

The guys looked at each other when Andrew mentioned their criminal activity.

"I was just thinking," Andrew continued quickly. "I've got a car. What if I drove while you guys did your thing? I could take you anywhere you want—you know the places. I just drive, and that's it."

Andrew watched while they thought about it. It didn't take long for them to decide to give him a chance. In fact, they told him to meet them later that night.

At the appointed time, Andrew picked them up in his car. They were armed with guns and masks, and as Andrew drove them through the city streets with rap music bottoming out the bass in his speakers, he felt unbreakable.

"Up there, on the right," one of the guys in the back seat yelled into his ear.

Andrew pulled into the convenience store parking lot and waited while the guys jumped out of the car. Less than two minutes later they were back in the car with cash, and Andrew peeled out of the parking lot.

One of the guys slapped him on the shoulder. "You're all right, man," he said with a grin.

The night was productive. Convenience stores. Apartment buildings. Gas stations. At the end of the night when Andrew dropped them off, they put a wad of cash in his hands. His cut was way more than he could have gotten on his own, but Andrew wasn't addicted to the money. He was addicted to the rush—the perverse thrill of adrenaline that was far beyond anything he had ever experienced.

The next night Andrew went out with the guys again.

One of the guys tried to hand him a gun. "Want to try?" he asked.

Andrew shook his head. He wanted to steal, but he was afraid he wouldn't be able to deal with the kind of intensity it required to actually put a gun in someone's face and demand money. Maybe someday, but not now. Not yet.

Andrew was getting home later and later. His parents tried to confront him about it, but he told them to mind their own business. When his dad told him it *was* his business to know where his son was at all hours of the night, Andrew put his fist through the wall.

"Stay out of my face," Andrew shouted at them. "Stay out of my room, and stay out of my life. The next time I use my fist, it won't just be on my wall."

They were afraid of him, and that's how Andrew wanted it. He could control them that way. The fear in their eyes fed his aggression, and as long as they wondered if he would hurt them, he was in charge. He could take that fear and lead them around on it like a leash.

Night after night Andrew's car appeared at specified locations around town, and the four guys would jump in with guns and masks. At the end of the night he would drop them off and go home. It wasn't a friendship; it was a business partnership. There was almost a professional distance between them, which was fine with Andrew. The only things he had in common with them were a broken conscience and a primal instinct for crime.

The convenience stores were always the same. The guys would run in with ski masks, hold the cashier at gunpoint, and demand money from the register. Of course, the cashier would do whatever they asked. They'd jump into the car with the cash and guns, and Andrew would speed away from the scene before the police were even called. The cashiers seemed to know that their best chance of surviving the robbery was to do exactly what they were told, and all of them did. All of them except one.

It was a drizzly night, and Andrew had picked up the guys from their usual place. They had already hit one small grocery store without incident. Andrew pulled the car up to a second convenience store and left the engine idling while the guys slipped on their ski masks, put the guns in their jackets, and jumped out of the car.

Andrew waited behind the wheel as the seconds ticked by. Adrenaline pumping, he looked in his mirrors, acutely aware of every car that passed. *Why aren't they out of there yet?* he wondered. *They should be done by now.* Nervously he tapped his fingers on the steering wheel. Something must have gone wrong. He tried to see in through the windows of the store. He could tell that there was a commotion going on, but he couldn't see what was happening.

Suddenly a piercing siren screamed in loud, rhythmic bursts from the store. An alarm. *Someone hit the button,* Andrew thought frantically. *The police will be here any second. Come on, come on, come on,* he pleaded. He looked around, wondering how he'd respond when cop cars came pouring into the parking lot. He couldn't leave them there. He couldn't drive away without them, and yet he knew they were seconds away from being caught.

Just then he saw the first masked figure running from the store, followed closely by the other three. They yanked the car doors open and jumped inside. "Go! Go! Go!" they shouted.

Andrew slammed the car into reverse and squealed the tires as the car whipped around backward, then locked into drive and sped away from the scene, bouncing over the curb and into traffic. As soon as the store was out of view, Andrew slowed to a normal speed and looked into his rearview mirror to see if anyone was following them. He blended into the flow of traffic and changed lanes.

"What happened in there?" he asked, alternately wiping each palm on his jeans.

"Stupid girl, man. Instead of just giving us the money, she freaked out. I mean, freaked out—screaming and trying to fight. She hit the button, and the alarm went off. It was all we could do to grab the money and get out of there. She slowed down when I cracked her across the face with the butt of my pistol, though. I think next time she'll do what she's told."

Just ahead they heard sirens blaring. "Here come the police," Andrew said. One after another, police cars whizzed past them, lights flashing, heading toward the convenience store they had just left. Andrew counted them as they zoomed past. *One, two, three . . . five, six, seven . . .*

"There were seven cop cars headed to where we just came from," Andrew said as they merged onto the freeway. He had an idea. "You know what that means, right? Every cop in this area is busy."

"And?" Dre said.

"And since all the cops are busy, what's stopping us from taking the next exit and doing it again?"

Andrew swerved off onto the next exit and pulled up to the next gas station. The guys jumped out and ran inside. Moments later they were back with a wad of cash. Andrew pulled out of the station. No cops in sight. This was too easy.

Andrew's private bankroll was getting fatter. Every night he came home with more money. The petty theft he had been involved with before seemed like child's play.

With Halloween fast approaching, Andrew noticed his neighbor's yards evolve into graveyards with fake tombstones and giant spiderwebs. Ghosts made of sheets swayed in the breeze from tree branches, and strings of orange lights appeared in the bushes. Soon the streets would be filled with miniature witches, fairies, monsters, cops, robbers . . . *robbers*. An idea began percolating in Andrew's head. *Everyone opens their doors to masked strangers on Halloween. Any home with lights on would easily be a potential target.*

The other guys liked the idea of using Halloween to their advantage. In fact, Dre told them about a couple of drug houses that would be perfect targets for a Halloween robbery. That's where they would seriously clean up. There would be not only money but also drugs and guns. And drug dealers don't call the cops when they're robbed.

Andrew could feel the thrill of an impending adventure begin to pulse through him. This would be the biggest exploit they'd ever attempted, and the danger level was ratcheted higher than it had ever been. He knew that Dre was right—drug dealers didn't call the police when they were robbed. They had other methods of handling their business, and those could turn deadly. They'd have to plan their moves carefully.

The night of October 31 was clear and cold. A hint of fog softened the streetlights as Andrew left his house. For once it wasn't raining, and Andrew was glad about that as he drove several blocks to the meeting place and nervously pulled his Thunderbird into the driveway. The guys came out of the house with gloves on and their weapons concealed under their coats. The passenger door opened. They popped the seat forward, and three of them slid into the back seat. Alan took shotgun, and Andrew shifted the car into reverse.

"The masks are in the back," Andrew told them.

The guys reached into the bag and pulled out the masks Andrew had picked up from a costume store. When they had slipped the masks over their heads, Andrew looked around the car to see the faces of Richard Nixon, Yogi Bear, a clown, and the devil.

"Turn up the music," the devil said.

Andrew reached down and turned the volume knob up. Music poured out of the speakers and filled the car. Bass rumbled in the throats of the subwoofers, and the windows rattled with the beat. The double-clicking sound of someone chambering a round punctuated the rhythm, while the voice chanted a hypnotic phrase: *Kill, kill, kill, murder, murder, murder . . .*

Andrew could feel the rhythm take over his body. It energized him. "Where are we going?" he asked.

"Turn left up here," Dre said.

There was something different in the air tonight. Andrew could sense it—a strange, electric feeling that made the hairs on his arms stand up. He couldn't figure out exactly what was out of the ordinary, but he knew things were about to change. That probably explained both the lure of excitement and the dark sense of foreboding that sloshed in his stomach. For a split second he thought about turning around.

Instead, taking a deep breath, Andrew flipped on his blinker, looked in his rearview mirror one last time, and turned the corner.

Chapter 7

Andrew sat in the getaway vehicle with the engine running. Behind his car a plume of exhaust swirled into the cold night air. He couldn't see what was happening in the house on the other side of the hedges, but it was taking a long time. A pair of headlights appeared down the narrow street, and Andrew held his breath as another car passed him on the left. He watched in his rearview mirror as brake lights brightened for a moment and then disappeared around the corner. He'd been looking over his shoulder all night, especially after they'd cut out of the drug houses with the money, guns, and drugs, afraid that an angry dealer out for revenge would figure out who they were and hunt them down. *There's no way they could know who we are,* he reassured himself. *They'd have to be psychic.*

They had driven past this house a couple of times to make sure some-one was home before they stopped. It was getting late, and this was their fourth residential target of the night, not including the drug houses they'd raided. At the first house the guy had opened the garage door thinking his wife was home, and instead met four guys with guns. At the second house the guy actually offered them candy before he realized what was happen-ing. They'd forced him back inside at gunpoint. At the third house a woman answered the door, obviously expecting little kids in costumes. Of course, she was surprised to see four men in masks instead.

The fourth house was on a side street tucked behind an untidy wall of greenery. When he saw people-shaped shadows moving in front of the window, Andrew slowly pulled the car over into the graveled shoulder. "They may not open the door this late. Let's go to the side and see if the patio door is unlocked," someone said from the back seat, and the four masked figures slipped out of the car and into the yard.

The home invasions were more lucrative when people were there, be-cause their cash and credit cards were home with them. People would also willingly direct them to their valuables, which saved time. It was amazing how helpful people became when they were being held at gunpoint in their living rooms and their phone cords had been ripped out of the walls. People spent their lives working to accumulate things, but in the telltale moment of choice they wisely traded their things for their lives. Oh, the irony.

To Andrew's knowledge, nobody had ever been shot during their outings, although he knew the guys used their pistols as weapons in other violent ways. When they were satisfied they had found everything they were looking for, the guys would lock the victims in the bathroom and tell them to count to 100. By the time they finished counting, Andrew and his partners were in the car and blocks away, a needle blending nicely into the proverbial haystack.

Andrew was feeling antsy in the driver's seat as he waited, looking over his shoulder at the fourth house, not knowing what was happening inside its walls. *These guys are pros,* he reminded himself. *They know what they're doing, and they know when to abort if they need to. Relax.*

In the sky a waxing crescent moon glowed above the crisscrossing power lines, highlighting the edges of wispy clouds. A procession of garbage cans and recycle bins stood watch along the edge of the driveway, and kids' toys were scattered on the lawn. *Kids live here,* Andrew thought. He turned the heater up and blew hot breath into his hands before rubbing them together. He wasn't sure what the temperature was, but he guessed it had dropped below 30 degrees. A chilly night for trick-or-treating.

A slight movement across the street in the neighbor's house caught his eye. He didn't see anyone, but a curtain dropped back into place and waved back and forth slightly. That was not good. Someone had been watching from the window. "Hurry up," he whispered, tapping the steering wheel.

Suddenly a masked face appeared at the passenger window, the door opened, and everyone piled in.

Andrew gunned it back onto the side street. "I think somebody was watching us back there," he said. "I saw a curtain move in the house across the street. We've got to get out of here. It's getting late anyway, so our trick-or-treating ruse isn't going to work anymore."

"We don't have any more room back here," Richard Nixon said, pulling his mask off. "The floorboard is full, and we have more on our laps. Let's call it a night."

"We have room for one more thing," the clown said, looking out the window at a guy walking down the street. He was carrying what looked like a huge bag of candy. "Pull the car over!"

Andrew swerved to the side of the road, and the masked clown jumped out. He punched the guy in the face and in the stomach a few times and grabbed the bag of candy before jumping back in the car. "Trick or treat!" he yelled at the guy lying on the sidewalk. He slammed the door, and they sped away.

"Candy, anybody?" the clown laughed as they cruised down Pacific Avenue. The streets had emptied of trick-or-treaters, and even on the main drag, businesses and residences had darkened for the night. He handed Andrew a lollipop and threw a handful of assorted candies at the other guys. "*Now* we can go home."

Andrew peeled off the wrapping and put the lollipop in his mouth, his mind and body still buzzing from the adrenaline. *What a night,* he thought. *We'll have to rob a bank to top this one.*

The trunk was full of thousands of dollars in cash, drugs, and guns, not to mention the jewelry, credit cards, and other valuables they'd acquired during the home invasions. The street price of the stolen items would be less than actual value, of course, but the overall take was massive for one night out.

Andrew glanced down at the digital clock, numbers glowing like un-blinking crimson eyes from the dashboard: *Exactly 11:30.* His parents were probably waiting up to lecture him about being out late on a school night. They'd probably threaten to take away his car or something stupid like that. Just for that, he might stay out even later. He already knew what he would say. It was Halloween, he'd tell them, as if it were any of their business. He was out with friends, trick-or-treating. That's probably all he'd need to say. He already knew they weren't going to push him that hard. They were afraid to.

"This is our turn, up here," Dre said, sucking on a piece of candy.

"I know," Andrew said. He slowed as they approached the intersection of 161st and Pacific Avenue, and put on his blinker. A moment later, in the middle of his turn, the street lit up in a sea of flashing red and blue lights—police cars converged on them from every direction. Police officers emerged from the cars, weapons drawn. They were trapped. Andrew gripped the steering wheel, trying to stay calm. His rib cage held his lungs captive, and he couldn't breathe. Blinding white floodlights illuminated the interior of the car.

"Be cool, everybody," Dre said quietly as the others cursed under their breath. "Don't move." He looked at Andrew. "Just roll down your window and talk to them, and stay cool."

Andrew carefully rolled down his window as officers approached the vehicle. "Driver, throw your keys out the window and put your hands in the air!" the officer shouted.

Andrew held the keys out the window and tossed them onto the frozen asphalt. The officer came up to the window warily and looked inside at each of them. "What are you doing out at this time of night?" he asked.

Swallowing, Andrew answered. "It's Halloween. We're trick-or-treating. See?" Andrew pointed to the bag of candy they had stolen from the guy on the street.

The officer shined his flashlight at the candy, and then into the back seat, illuminating the piles of stolen goods, including the masks. "Trick-or-treating, huh? With Richard Nixon and the devil?"

A moment later Andrew tasted frosty asphalt as the officer, in one smooth motion, had thrown the car door open and forcefully pulled him out from behind the wheel, pushing him to the ground and pressing his face against the street. Andrew then felt the cold metal of a pair of handcuffs as they were tightened around his wrists. They searched him, examined his identification, and then deposited him in the back of a police car. From his limited vantage point, Andrew saw that they'd put each of the guys into a separate squad car. He watched helplessly while the police opened the Thunderbird's trunk and discovered the weapons, drugs, and cash. Andrew cursed under his breath.

When the officer walked back over to the squad car and opened the door, Andrew already knew what he was going to say. "Andrew Michell, you are under arrest. You have the right to remain silent."

Andrew tried to think. He'd been arrested before, but never with a trunk full of incriminating evidence against him. If only he had taken a different route. Or driven faster. Or turned sooner.

"Anything you say can and will be used against you in a court of law. You have the right to an attorney. If you cannot afford an attorney, one will be provided for you."

He was still a minor. If he just confessed to driving the car, they might go easy on him. What was one more night in Remann Hall? He knew the drill. By the time they booked him and finished filing the paperwork, he'd sleep a little, eat breakfast, and probably be out of there tomorrow morning.

"Do you understand the rights I just read to you?" the officer continued.

Andrew nodded.

"With these rights in mind, do you wish to speak to me?"

Andrew took a deep breath.

Chapter 8

Andrew sat on the bed with his back up against the cement block wall. Three rectangles of light came in through the tiny windows above him and stretched across the opposite wall of his cell—a wall consisting of 132 cement blocks painted the color of regurgitated buttermilk. Beneath him a stained, emaciated mattress put an inch or two of skimpy comfort between him and the wooden bed frame. He'd been staring at the same wall for two days, replaying his confession again and again in his mind. His confession was a formality, really; he'd already been caught red-handed.

Even after he'd confessed to driving the car, Andrew had to endure sitting in a hard chair in an isolated room with his hands cuffed together while the officers came at him with angled questions. But their questions didn't make sense. He had no idea what they were talking about. Why were the police so interested in the guns and other crimes? His back hurt, and he felt as if his eyes were scorching under the bright lights. He was exhausted.

"I drove the car," Andrew had told them again and again. "That's it. I don't know anything else."

Then they had started asking him other questions—questions that were even more confusing, dealing with a string of unsolved murders that had recently taken place in the area. Andrew was stunned. He was a thief, not a murderer. They kept asking him questions about the other guys. Why would they be asking him about his partners in crime and . . . murder? He knew they were dangerous; he just wasn't sure how dangerous. But he was glad he didn't know.

"I don't *know* anything," Andrew had said helplessly.

Finally they had taken him to a cell and left him there. As Andrew sat on the hard mattress thinking, he secretly began to wonder if any of the guys he'd been spending time with *was* capable of murder. He knew they were dangerous; he just wasn't sure how dangerous. He was glad he didn't know.

I wonder why my parents haven't picked me up yet, Andrew thought. *Must be trying to teach me a lesson or something.* He stood and walked over to look out through the bars. The noise was enough to make a guy go crazy. The constant talking, yelling, and cursing from the other young prisoners and the blaring TV gave Andrew a headache. The place was a circus. *I'm going to have so much homework to do when I get out of here.*

"Michell!" a guard said. "You've got a visitor. Let's go."

Finally, Andrew thought.

It was evening, the only time family members were allowed to visit. They led Andrew to the visiting area, where his parents were waiting. He walked toward them, and they stood up. "He looks terrible," he heard his mom whisper to his dad.

"So," Andrew said when they sat down. "What's happening? When do I get out of here?"

His dad looked incredulous. "Andrew, do you have any idea the seriousness of what you've done?" he said. "They called us at 4:00 a.m. to tell us they had arrested you, and the next day it was all over the news. We found out on the news report that the police had been looking for you guys for weeks before they finally caught up to you. "

"It was on the news?" Andrew asked, surprised. "Well, so what's going to happen? When can I come home?"

Andrew's dad started to cry. "Andrew, don't you get it? You're not coming home. You're going to be in jail for a long time. They said on the news that they are cracking down on young people committing violent crimes. As a minor, you could be in jail until you're 21. That's *if* they charge you as a minor. If they decide to charge you as an adult . . ." His dad didn't finish the sentence. Instead, he shook his head and stared at his hands.

Andrew sat back in his chair and stared blankly at nothing. *Five years?*

"We're working on getting you an attorney," his mom said.

Andrew barely heard anything else they said. He couldn't imagine being in jail for five years. Two days staring at that blank wall had almost driven him crazy. If he had to look at it for five years . . .

Back in his cell, Andrew felt claustrophobic as the reality of his situation finally closed in around him and smothered him in panic. The tears finally fell, making wet lines all over his face. Reality was sinking in, and he was scared. He couldn't survive five years in a place such as this. This was serious—more serious than he had ever imagined. His life was over. And it was only going to get worse.

★★★

Monte Hester, of the Hester Law Group, was a well-known trial attorney with white hair and lines of experience in his face. He and his associate attorney, Wayne Fricke, both wore glasses and serious expressions. They sat across the table from Andrew and let him digest the news they had just told him: the prosecutor had decided to charge him as an adult.

Mr. Hester leaned forward. "Andrew, when you were arrested, did you say anything to the police?"

Andrew nodded. "Yeah, I confessed to what I did."

Mr. Hester sighed, and a knowing look passed between him and Mr. Fricke. Andrew read the look easily: any chance he might have had was shot when he confessed. His was an open-and-shut case. Andrew told them everything he could think of about the night of the robberies. His attorneys promised to do what they could to defend him, and the conversation ended. Andrew was escorted back to his cell to wait.

Andrew had been in solitary confinement during his first few days in custody, but on the day of his arraignment, he was shackled to about 30 other prisoners wearing matching orange-colored pumpkin suits. The guards placed them in a holding cell, where they sat and waited together. The group of prisoners made up a dull mosaic of degraded humanity, strung together by chains and circumstances. The overpowering collective stench was a mix of ripe body odor with a hint of alcoholic vomit. Andrew tried not to breathe or make eye contact as he furtively looked around the room. He knew he probably didn't smell that great himself.

All of the men were older than he was, probably by at least 10 years. Some of the men seemed resigned or even bored; others chewed on dirty fingernails or tapped their feet on the concrete floor. All of them kept looking in his direction. Andrew realized with growing unease that he was the center of attention.

Why do they keep looking at me? Andrew wondered. *What do they want?*

"Look at you!" the guy with the braid finally said. "You're just a little kid! What are you in for, stealing candy bars?"

The rest of the guys laughed, and Andrew shifted uncomfortably in his seat, his chains clanking in his lap.

"You gotta be, what, 130 pounds soaking wet? How old are you, anyway?"

"Sixteen," Andrew said, staring at the floor.

"Sixteen," the man echoed. "Unbelievable. What in the world did you do? What are you doing here with the big boys? Why aren't you in kiddie jail?"

Andrew didn't feel like talking, and was relieved when the guards made them stand up and file out of the holding cell. They were escorted to the courtroom to appear before the judge. Each prisoner's name was called, followed by the crime or list of crimes he was charged with committing. The crimes the other prisoners had been arrested for seemed minor in comparison to what Andrew knew he'd be facing. The others' crimes ranged from domestic violence to driving under the influence. When Andrew heard the judge call his name, he stood, hands cuffed and chained to his waist. All eyes in the courtroom were on him, and he could feel his face burning.

"Andrew Michell, you are hereby charged with the following crimes: Kidnapping in the first degree, count one. Kidnapping in the first degree, count two. Kidnapping in the first degree, count three . . ."

Andrew heard one of the prisoners quietly whistle between his teeth as the judge continued. The other prisoners were staring with their jaws open.

" . . . Kidnapping in the first degree, count seven. Armed robbery in the first degree, count one. Armed robbery in the first degree, count two . . ."

When the judge had finished listing his charges, Andrew pleaded not guilty, as instructed by his attorney. It was a formality, his attorney had told him. Everyone pleads not guilty at the arraignment. The judge ordered him held on $1 million bail.

When he got back to the holding cell, the other prisoners resumed staring at him. "What did you *do*?" the guy sitting next to him asked. "Are you crazy?"

Andrew shrugged.

"Do you even understand what this means?" another guy asked.

Andrew looked up. "What do you mean?"

"OK, when it comes to crimes, the court system has a seriousness scale. The most serious is first-degree, premeditated murder. The second most serious charge is kidnapping."

"Yes?" Andrew said slowly.

The man continued. "Seven counts of kidnapping, two burglaries, one residential burglary, and three armed robberies? You're looking at life behind bars, kid."

One of the guards joined in. "You're going to be here for at least 80 years," he said, shaking his head. "You'll never see the outside again. Hope you like the food. You're here for life."

Andrew couldn't stop his hands from shaking. One night's crime spree couldn't possibly cost him his entire life. Could it? *What have I done?* he thought. He didn't want to cry in front of these tough-looking older guys, so he bit his tongue and tried to concentrate on the variegated shades of gray concrete beneath his feet.

"You got a real attorney, or a public pretender?" the man with the braid asked.

"A real attorney," Andrew said. "He's supposed to be the best criminal defense attorney around."

"Good. 'Cause you're going to need one."

Back in solitary confinement, Andrew laid on his mattress, a motionless human lump. He could actually feel himself disappearing. The world outside was still turning, but inside these four walls it had stopped. His friends would go on to graduate from high school, date pretty girls, get jobs, get married, have kids, and build a life. He would never do any of those things. He was going to rot in prison.

He could already feel the rest of the world forgetting about him and moving on while he simply evaporated. He might as well be dead. Despair filled up every empty space inside him, and he turned his face to the wall. He wondered how many other prisoners had stared at this same wall and wished they could die.

Chapter 9

Feeling like a caged animal, Andrew paced back and forth the length of his cell, counting his steps. Twenty-three hours a day in solitary confinement was taking its toll on his mind. Most of the prisoners were sent to solitary for breaking the rules or causing trouble. As a minor, Andrew was in the hole for one reason: his own safety.

In solitary his only human interaction was at mealtime and the one hour per day he was allowed "recreation," which turned out to be a fancy description for getting out of his cell and walking around the waiting area. It beat sitting in his closet-sized space alone, though. At least during recreation he could pause at the doors of other cells and talk to other inmates. That's how he had met Walter, who lived in the next cell over from his.

Andrew heard the clanging of keys and turned around to see the guard unlocking his cell door. *Recreation time,* Andrew thought wryly as he walked out into the waiting area.

"Hey, Andy," Walter called to him from inside his own cell. Walter had been in general population, but he'd gotten into a fight and beat a guy up. The guards had tossed him in the hole—solitary confinement—to teach him a lesson. Walter told Andrew he didn't have a choice but to fight. That was the way to survive out there.

"Hi, Walter," Andrew said, peeking through the bars. "What's up?"

"Oh, you know, the same old thing. Trying to decide between veal Parmesan and rib-eye steak for dinner," Walter joked.

Andrew grinned. "I recommend the industrial-grade mystery meat. Chef's special."

Walter laughed, and then sobered as he looked through the bars at Andrew's face. "How are you holding up, kid?"

Andrew shrugged. "I don't know. It stinks, man. At home I had everything I ever wanted, you know? Now I've got nothing but four walls staring me down."

Walter studied him for a moment, and then turned to rustle through his things. "I got something here. I want you to have it. I think maybe you need it more than I do."

"What is it?" Andrew asked.

Reaching through the bars, Walter handed Andrew a book. Andrew looked down at the cover as he ran his finger over the embossed words. "A Bible?" he asked.

"Yeah," Walter said. "Somebody gave it to me, but I want you to have it. Keep it. It's a gift."

"Thanks."

Andrew had seen Bibles plenty of times before. His parents had a few different ones on the bookshelves at home, but he'd never read them. In fact, he didn't even remember his parents reading them. His mom and dad had taken him and his brothers to the old white Presbyterian church downtown before John had died, and he'd seen Bibles there, too. Of course, after John had died, they seemed to go to church only on special days, such as Easter and Christmas. Even then Andrew would sneak out of his class and go swipe candy bars from the corner store.

Now he was standing here holding Walter's Bible, a Gideon King James Version. It was nice of Walter to give him something. He decided to check it out when he got back to his cell.

"Oh, hey, Walter? One more thing," Andrew said. "I heard that they've let some of the other younger guys out of solitary and into general population. Any idea how I could get into general population? I'd rather be out there."

"No, you wouldn't," Walter corrected him. "A kid like you? They'd eat you alive. The other young guys are bigger than you. They've got tattoos. They look like criminals. But you? No way."

"I don't care," Andrew said. "I've got to get out of here. Tell me what to do. Can't I sign a waiver or something?"

"Look," Walter said. "I just spent 10 years in San Quentin. I've seen what happens to guys like you. Trust me. You do not want to be out there."

Andrew felt irritation warm his ears. How could Walter know what he did and did not want? "I don't care," he insisted.

Walter paused and looked at him. "You seem like a smart kid bookwise, but I think you may be lacking in street smarts." He sighed. "OK, here's what you have to do. You have to fill out a request form and send it to the lieutenant. You have to waive your right to safety, and they'll take you to population. Got it?"

Andrew grinned. *Finally, a way out of hell's basement,* he thought. "Thanks, Walter."

Walter shook his head.

Andrew submitted his request to the lieutenant, and went back to his cell with his Bible. He lay down on his thin mattress and opened the pages. He tried to read it, skimming through several chapters, but the words were written in some kind of old English language with a lot of "thees" and "thous" and "wherewiths."

What is this? Andrew thought. *It doesn't make any sense.* It made his brain hurt. He tried to remember something, anything, he'd learned from church or the church camp he'd gone to when he was little.

The Ten Commandments, he thought. *I remember hearing about the Ten Commandments!*

Andrew thumbed through the pages, but couldn't find anything resembling the Ten Commandments. He stood up and pounded on the wall of the cell next door. "Hey!" he called. "Aren't the Ten Commandments in the Bible? I want to read the Ten Commandments and find out what they say."

"Yeah," Walter called. "I think they're in the front somewhere."

In the front somewhere? That's not much help, Andrew thought. He thumbed through the pages for a while longer before he eventually closed the Bible and put it down. He was fascinated with the idea of it, especially since there were churches and pastors that seemed to hang on every word, but to Andrew it was gibberish.

The next day during Walter's recreation Andrew called him over to his cell. "Guess what?" Andrew announced when Walter's face appeared at the bars. "They're coming to get me. They're taking me to general population. I just got the news."

Walter looked somber. "OK, kid. Look, this is what is going to happen. Because you're so young, you're going to walk out there and look like a potential victim to the rest of the guys in prison. Someone is going to call you a name. Or someone is going to disrespect you. Or someone is going to steal something from you." Walter rested his fingers on the bars. "Listen up. This is important, Andy. The very moment they call you a name or steal something from you, you attack them. It doesn't matter who they are."

"Attack them?" Andrew asked.

"Yes," Walter continued. "Prison life is very primitive. It's very animalistic. You need to attack and show that you will fight. Otherwise, they are going to make your life a living hell. And if you get knocked down, don't stay down. Get back up. Always get back up."

Andrew grinned at Walter. "Walter, come on, man. Maybe that's the way it happens in the movies, but—"

Walter interrupted Andrew, and he wasn't laughing. "Trust me. I've been out there, Andy. I know what it's like. You have to show them you will fight. And there's another unwritten rule in prison—a code of conduct. Listen to me, Andy. When there's something going on, such as a fight, you mind your own business. Don't watch the fight, don't look that direction, and don't ever, ever snitch to the guards about anything you've seen or heard. Guys have been killed for less than that."

It was late in the evening when the guards came to get Andrew. All he had to take with him was his blanket and his Bible. He gathered his two possessions and waved as he walked past Walter's cell. Walter nodded at him as though he were a dead man walking.

"Here you go. Welcome to population. Good luck," one of the guards said when they'd arrived.

Andrew stood in the general population tank holding his blanket and his Bible as the guards walked away. Several hundred guys were scattered through the room playing cards or exercising or talking. When they noticed Andrew, the room gradually became quiet. Swallowing stage fright, Andrew looked around at the unwelcoming faces of the older men.

Andrew suddenly felt like a high school football player subbed in to play quarterback for the Seattle Seahawks on NFL Sunday in front of a full stadium—he was definitely out of place among these big guys with protruding muscles and prison tattoos. He could tell they were wondering what in the world he was doing there. It was written on their faces.

"Hey," a voice said.

Andrew looked down to see a few guys playing cards at a nearby table.

"Hey. Sit down. We'll deal you in." One of the guys motioned to an empty chair.

Andrew slid into the chair and picked up the hand of cards they dealt him. Gradually the noise level began to rise again, and Andrew started breathing again. He hadn't realized he'd stopped.

The guys at the table watched him curiously. "Who are you?" the dealer asked. "Why are you in here?"

The other two guys stared at Andrew; the game momentarily paused while they waited for an answer.

"Seven kidnappings, three robberies, and two burglaries," Andrew said finally.

All three of the guys spit out expletives. "Whoa!" one of the guys said with a sinister laugh that sent chills down Andrew's spine. "That's insane! What were you thinking?"

Andrew shrugged.

"Is this your first time in general population?" the dealer asked.

"Yeah," Andrew said.

"Listen," the dealer continued. "I'm going to warn you. You're small and weak. When someone does something to you—and it will happen— you've got to fight back. If they take something from you or call you a name, don't back down. Fight. That piece of advice is free. Welcome to population."

The reality of Walter's advice began to sink in, and Andrew wondered if he had made a mistake, but it was too late now. He had signed a waiver.

That night there was a problem with overcrowding. All the cells were full, with two guys in each cell. The rest of the inmates, including Andrew, had to sleep on the floor. Andrew lay down with his blanket and his Bible while the guards locked down the area and dimmed the lights.

Andrew shifted around on the floor, trying to get comfortable under- neath his blanket.

"Hey, you!"

Andrew looked up and saw one of the prisoners in a cell looking through the bars at him. He looked like a slab of beef on legs; his large stubby fingers curled and uncurled around the bars. Andrew could tell from his tattoos that he was a gang member.

"Yeah, I'm talking to you, you little ———."

Andrew's ears burned, and he laid his head down while the man con- tinued to yell insults at him.

"You can't let him talk to you like that," the man next to Andrew said in a low voice. "Stick up for yourself, kid. If you don't, you'll pay for it."

"What do I say?" Andrew whispered.

The man rattled off a string of derogatory phrases for Andrew to say.

Andrew repeated them loudly, and the beast behind bars became en- raged, throwing verbal counterattacks at Andrew.

Some of the other prisoners began to egg Andrew on. "Psst! Tell him this! Tell him this!" Encouraged by the other guys, Andrew boldly re- peated the insults they told him to say.

The man in the cell stared him down. "You're talking big now, kid. In a few hours when the lights come on and the cell doors open, we'll see how big your ego is. You and me. Tomorrow morning."

He disappeared into the darkness of his cell, and Andrew lay on the floor, shivering slightly under his blanket. Realization crept over him, and tiny chills shot through his body. He'd had words with one of the mean- est-looking guys in the tank, and there was only one way it could be re- solved: violence. Andrew wasn't much of a fighter. He had been in fights before with people his own age, but this—this was a whole different brand of intensity.

As the night wore on, most of the other prisoners went to sleep, but Andrew couldn't even close his eyes. His stomach was in knots, and he could feel cold sweat on his skin. His dad wasn't there to defend him. He had no friends to back him up, no one to watch out for him. He was alone. Well, almost.

Andrew reached under his mat and pulled out the Bible that Walter had given him. He opened the front pages and tried to make out the words in the dim light. His eyes hurt as he worked to focus on the page in front of him. He could barely read the headings on the first page: "For promises of forgiveness. For promises of comfort. For promises of hope." Each heading was followed by a list of text references, but Andrew couldn't read them.

Man, I need this! Andrew thought, tears burning on the inside of his eyelids. *There's got to be something magical in here that will help me! Where is the hope?* He wondered if somewhere the God this Bible talked about knew what was happening. Maybe He was listening. Just in case, Andrew whispered some words of desperation. "I don't know what's in this Bible. I feel as though something in here could help me, but I don't even know where to look."

It wasn't an official prayer, like the ones his mom had said at Thanksgiving, but it was the best Andrew could do.

Andrew slid the Bible back under his mat and curled up with his blanket under his chin. The night's remaining seconds ticked silently by while Andrew lay in a pool of his own sweat, waiting for morning. He must have fallen asleep, because he awakened to bright lights blinking on and the echoing sounds of cell doors unlocking. The time had come.

Chapter 10

As soon as the guard had finished unlocking the cell doors and walked away to the next pod, the inmate Andrew had argued with the night before began stalking toward him, parting a sea of other prisoners on his way to where Andrew stood. Andrew knew there was no place to hide. Walter had warned him that he would have to fight and that there was no way out of this situation, except through his own fists. He clenched his fingers into his palms as the man drew nearer.

"You had a lot to say last night, you little ——," the prisoner said as he moved into Andrew's personal space and called him a name. The man towered over him, shoulders back, with hands balled into fat fists. "Let's see what you have to say now!"

Attack him, Andrew told himself. *Show them you will fight.*

Andrew tightened his body and lunged toward him, but the inmate's experienced fist met him on the cheek like a sledgehammer on asphalt. Andrew sprawled backward and slid across the floor as fireworks went off in his head. He writhed on the concrete floor, nauseated. The room spun circles around him.

Get up. Andrew could almost hear Walter coaching him in his mind. *No matter what happens, you gotta get up. Don't ever stay down.*

Andrew tried to focus, but his vision blurred with each pounding pulse in his head. He pushed himself up off the floor and turned to face his opponent on shaky legs. He could feel his left eye swelling shut, but he knew he had no choice. He couldn't quit.

Andrew choked on terror as he looked at the man's eyes. They didn't look human.

In every other situation Andrew had always felt invincible. He thought it was funny when his parents and other people were afraid of him, but here no one was afraid of him. And here there was no referee and no bell. Just a primitive fight for survival with prison rules, and it wasn't over. Andrew gritted his teeth and lunged again.

This time the fist met him on the other cheek, and Andrew could feel the reverberation through his skull. Like a striking rattlesnake, the fist bit him a second, third, fourth time, and he crumpled. A second later he blinked back to consciousness, his face on the cold floor. His body ached, and he wondered if anything was broken. It didn't matter. *You've got to get up,* he thought. *Can't stay down. You've got to fight.*

Through tiny, swollen slits for his eyes, Andrew could barely see that an audience of prison-issued shoes had gathered around him on the floor.

They're watching the fight? Andrew wondered. *I thought the unwritten rule was you never watch a fight in prison.* Apparently this particular throwdown was too entertaining to pass up. So much for the code of conduct.

Andrew pushed himself up onto his knees, and then slowly regained his balance. When he turned the other inmates, including his opponent, had scattered. A moment later he understood why.

"What's going on here?" a guard snapped, walking up to Andrew. He looked down at him, and his eyes grew wide. "What happened to your face?"

Andrew reached fingers up to his swollen cheeks. When he pulled them back, he could see they were covered in blood.

"I said, 'What happened to your face?'" the guard demanded.

Andrew looked around at the other inmates, who were now busy trying not to pay attention to what was happening. Andrew knew they were still listening, waiting to see if he would rat someone out.

Andrew squinted up at the guard. "Well," he said loudly, making sure the other prisoners could hear what he was saying. "I fell. I fell and hit my face on a doorknob."

The guard's mouth dropped open. "A doorknob did that to your face?"

"Yep," Andrew said. His head pounded like a jackhammer. He wanted to throw up.

The guard shook his head. "Come with me," he said. The other prisoners sneaked cautious glances in his direction as Andrew picked up his blanket and his Bible and limped painfully after the guard. He knew the guard was well aware that he was lying. First, there was no way a doorknob could have done that much damage. Second, there were no doorknobs in general population.

The guard took him to another part of the jail in a separate tank on a different floor. When Andrew finally reached the new holding area, he lay down on the floor, curled up, and closed his eyes. After a sleepless night and a brutal lesson in prison etiquette, Andrew wanted nothing more than to be left alone to rest and heal. Mercifully, drowsiness took over, and Andrew drifted off to sleep.

The voices sounded as if they were far away at first, then gradually, as Andrew became aware of his surroundings, the din of a TV and clanking dishes and voices talking grew louder.

"Wow, look at that guy's face," he heard someone say. "Somebody really messed him up."

Andrew tried to open his eyes and move, but his body felt as if it was trapped under a semi. His eyes were sticky, and he could taste blood. He could smell food, but he wasn't hungry. He knew people were looking at him and could hear them commenting on his appearance, but Andrew just lay there on the floor, too beat-up to care.

"Michell! Michell!"

Across the room a guard was yelling over the heads of a couple hundred prisoners. "Got a package for Michell!" he called. The guard was pronouncing his last name MITCH-ell, instead of how it was supposed to be pronounced, like the girl's name Michelle.

Oh, well, Andrew thought, wincing. *It's probably better if I'm not known in prison as "Michelle," anyway.* He might have worked up the energy for a cynical laugh if it hadn't been so painful. In his condition there was no way he was going to be able to get up and walk down to receive a package. Come to think of it, he had no idea why he would be receiving a package.

One of the other prisoners realized Andrew was too injured to walk the distance, so he retrieved the package and brought it over to him. "Here ya go, buddy."

Andrew reached up and took the package. He could barely see through his swollen eyes, but he was curious as to the contents of the package, so he opened it up and looked inside. It was a book. He pulled it out and examined it, holding it close to his face so he could read the words on the front with his limited vision. It was another Bible—the New Living Translation, Andrew looked at the note and discovered that his mom had gone to a bookstore, ordered this translation of the Bible, and had it mailed to him in prison.

But I've only been here five days. How could she have ordered it and had it shipped so soon? Andrew thought. He then realized that this Bible had arrived only a few hours after his first attempt at a prayer for help. Was it a coincidence? Or did Someone . . . God . . . arrange for the answer to his prayer before he'd ever prayed it? God must have impressed his mom to buy it and send it to him. A nervous tingle fluttered through Andrew's stomach. He looked down at the razor-thin pages and breathed in the smell of the new leather binding. He had a strange feeling that it was a message—that Someone was trying to tell him something. Lying on the cold floor shivering in pain, Andrew decided that if that was the case, maybe he should listen.

That same day the lieutenant and the other jail staff made the decision to put all of the juveniles at Pierce County Jail into solitary confinement for their own safety. Andrew's entire experience with general population lasted less than a day, and he was back in solitary confinement.

Once again Andrew sat in his tiny cell on his flat mattress. But for the moment he was worse off than he had been before. Although bored and lonely in solitary confinement, before going to general population he had at least had his face intact. Now he had a couple of black eyes, a fat lip, a pounding headache, and *still* nothing to do. Nothing to do, that is, except read his brand-new Bible. He randomly opened the pages and started reading from the book of Proverbs, chapter 1, and verse 1.

"These are the proverbs of Solomon, David's son, king of Israel," Andrew read silently, thankful that the simple words weren't tangled up in "thees" and "thous." He read on. *"The purpose of these proverbs is to teach people wisdom and discipline, and to help them understand wise sayings. Through these proverbs, people will receive instruction in discipline, good conduct, and doing what is right, just, and fair. These proverbs will make the simpleminded clever. They will give knowledge and purpose to young people."*

That's exactly what I need, Andrew thought, sitting alone in his cell. *I need knowledge. I need wisdom. I need a purpose.*

For the first time since his incarceration Andrew experienced something stirring inside him, something that kind of felt like hope. Maybe there *was* more to life than just being born and dying. Determined to know the truth, Andrew turned the page of his new Bible and kept reading.

Chapter 11

Wintertime pinched daylight into a few short hours between sunrise and sunset, but inside Andrew's cell in solitary confinement little changed, and the hours continued to stretch into what seemed like years. His only escape came when he opened the pages of his Bible and became engrossed in the words. During those times, although his body was still in prison, his mind was free to learn and explore a new and fascinating world.

As he delved into Scripture, something strange began happening inside him. It started in his head with the knowledge that his actions were actually morally wrong. If he'd been able to follow the advice of Solomon in Proverbs when he was younger, he wouldn't be staring at the same four walls in prison right now. *Listen to your parents. Don't make friends with fools. Don't be enticed by things that are attractive but deadly.* He had done exactly the opposite.

Then he read the book of Matthew and absorbed the life of Jesus. As he read the stories of Jesus, who knew what His purpose was and went around healing and teaching people and then willingly died a horrific death, that knowledge began to trickle from Andrew's head to his heart. He felt emotions he never remembered feeling before—emotions that twisted his conscience into a painful vise of guilt and remorse. When he started reading the Bible, he had been looking for encouragement and hope. Instead, he found words of cutting pain. One day he read Jeremiah 23:29, which resonated with his experience of reading the Bible: *"Does not my word burn like fire?"* asks the Lord. *"Is it not like a mighty hammer that smashes rock to pieces?"*

Sometimes when he closed his eyes at night, though, memories of terrible things he had done played back in his mind, taunting him, accusing him, condemning him. But it wasn't the voice he felt speaking to his mind from the Bible—the voice that showed him his guilt and offered a way out at the same time. This voice was different. He could have sworn it was the same powerful force that had compelled him to steal and destroy and had landed him in prison. Now the voice was coming back to point a bony finger at him for the very acts it had inspired and to try to destroy him again, only this time it wanted to destroy him with guilt. He thought of Jesus in the wilderness with the devil tempting him again and again and how Jesus had been able to resist. He could imagine what the devil's voice sounded like. He was pretty sure he'd heard it. *If only I had been able to resist the way that Jesus did,* Andrew thought.

It wasn't until he read the book of Romans that he realized that the worst thing he had done wasn't driving a getaway car for armed robbers or stealing from every store in the mall or threatening to hurt his parents. The worst thing he had done was living a life that didn't have God in it. All of his hatred and crimes were just symptoms of a godless existence. Andrew wondered what his life would have looked like, what his purpose would have been, if he had known then what he knew now. For Andrew, it was like standing in front of the floodgates of a dam and getting slammed by a massive, overwhelming tsunami of conviction. It was a shocking, violent process.

Andrew had hated his dad for showing emotion, but now he was the one crying his eyes out. Every time he read the Bible he found himself so moved that he couldn't hold back the tears. He watched as they dripped off his nose and puddled on the floor underneath him. For once he was thankful that he was in solitary confinement and didn't have a cellmate there to watch him fall apart.

"Look, God, I don't know anything about the Bible," Andrew said out loud one day as he knelt down in his cell and prayed. "I don't know anything about You. I just know that I've ruined my life. I've ruined the life of my friends. I've ruined the life of my family. And I just want You to know before I die in prison . . . I just want You to know that I'm sorry for what I did. I don't know how this all goes, but if it's possible, I want You to forgive me."

Springtime came, but to Andrew the only real difference was that the rectangles of light on the wall coming in through the tiny windows above him lingered longer. He imagined that the trees were starting to bloom and blustery showers were awakening flowers and painting the lawns a vibrant shade of green. He wished he could see it. He wished he could smell it. But unfortunately he wasn't going anywhere.

In April, five long months after his arrest, Andrew received the news. He would finally face his criminal charges and receive his sentence. But the prosecutors seemed willing to negotiate.

"We're going to offer you a plea bargain," the prosecutor told Andrew and his attorney. "If you go to trial, you know you're going to lose, and you're going to spend the rest of your life in prison. However, if you plead guilty to the robberies and burglaries with a gun enhancement, we'll drop the kidnapping charges. You're looking at a sentence range of 13 to 15 years."

Andrew knew the prosecutor was right about what would happen if he went to trial. On the advice of his attorney, he accepted the plea bargain. Shortly thereafter, he stood in a courtroom in front of a judge and waited to hear the decision. The judge sentenced him to 147 months in prison—12 years, three months.

Two days later Andrew was transferred to the Washington Corrections Center in Shelton, where he was placed in another solitary confinement cell. But this was a short-term location until they determined where he'd serve out his sentence.

At the prison in Shelton, Andrew's existence was even more isolated than before. He was starting over. He didn't know anyone, and he had little contact with any other humans. He was alone with his thoughts, which were sometimes his friends and sometimes his enemies.

Nothing ever happened in solitary confinement. He felt as if he repeated the same day again and again in the same cell. Andrew tried to see it as a good thing—at least he had a lot of time alone to read—but sometimes it was hard to be optimistic. He spent most of his time reading his Bible.

Three times a day Andrew heard the squeaky wheels of the meal cart as it rolled through the corridor. He waited for the squeaking to stop in front of his cell and then anticipated the tray of food that was slid into his cell. Not that the food was exciting; it wasn't. Most of the time it was some sort of unrecognizable meat from a mystery animal, a stale piece of white bread, weird cheese that wouldn't melt, and some peanut butter that had been sitting on a shelf somewhere for so long it was hard and crusty. But mealtime was simply something to do. It was an event. Actually, besides his parents' visits, it was really the only event that broke up the monotony of his day.

Let's see, Andrew thought, thumbing through his Bible. *What will I read about today?*

Andrew found a book in the Bible called "Daniel." It looked interesting, so he started to read. As the story unfolded, Andrew felt himself drawn into the dramatic plot. Daniel, a young man who came from a high-ranking family, was taken captive along with some of his friends by an army from a rival kingdom. He spent the first three years of his captivity learning a new language, reading literature, and preparing to serve in the king's palace. They changed everything about him—his name, his language, his home—but there was one thing Daniel would not let them change: his food. Even though the palace offered all kinds of fancy delicacies and rich meats, Daniel insisted on eating a simple diet of vegetables.

That's weird, Andrew thought. *I wonder why food was such a big deal to him.*

Andrew continued to read. The chief official of the palace was worried. It was his job to make sure that Daniel and the others had the best royal food so they would stay healthy. Daniel convinced the chief official to let them eat vegetables and drink water for 10 days, and then test them against the young men who had eaten the fancy royal food. After 10 days Daniel and his friends were healthier than the others. The chief official let them continue their simple diet.

"Hey, are you going to come get your food tray or what?" the guard yelled.

Andrew looked up, startled. He was so engrossed in the story of Daniel that he hadn't even heard the squeaky meal cart rolling by. He walked over, picked up his tray, and looked at the food on it. *Does what I eat really make that much difference in my health and appearance?* Andrew wondered. *If so, I wonder what difference it would make for my mind.*

Andrew wanted to know more about what made up a healthy diet. He decided he would keep his eyes open for books on the subject any time books became available in the prison. In the meantime, he decided, he could at least drink water and exercise in his cell.

Andrew didn't stop reading even to eat lunch. He couldn't put the Bible down. Each chapter of Daniel seemed to be more important than the one before; he'd never read anything more compelling. His mind was enraptured with Daniel's interpreting important dreams and the secrets of the future that were hidden in the mysterious symbols. He was anxious to know how it would end, but he was surprised to get to the final chapters of the book and learn that the words of the prophetic mystery would be sealed until the time of the end.

The time of the end? What is that? Andrew tried to process everything he had read. *If only I had someone to help me understand all of this.*

"Michell! You have visitors!" a guard called.

Andrew put his Bible down and backed up against the door of his cell with his hands behind him. He reached through the cuff port while the guard cuffed his hands together. Two guards escorted him down a long hallway to a room where he sat down and looked at his parents through the bulletproof glass.

For the first time in his life, Andrew could see them—really see them—as people. There they were, faithfully coming to see their only remaining son at every opportunity. During the past few months Andrew had begun to develop a relationship with them. He'd confessed things to them—things he had done that they'd never known about. They had reacted with shock. They had known only the tip of the iceberg when it came to Andrew's crimes, and each time they visited he had more to share. Finally one day, as he was about to get more off his chest, his mom had stopped him. "I don't want to know any more, Andrew," she said. "Please don't tell me any more."

Then Andrew's mom had made a confession of her own. "We were so relieved when we found out that you had been arrested," she said. "We had been so afraid that you were going to kill us, or yourself, or someone else."

Andrew shielded his parents from any more confessions after that. They talked only about positive things—what Andrew was learning, what was happening with his parents. His mom and dad told him that they were building another garage and that Lina came to see them often. Andrew felt good about that. He didn't like the idea of them being alone, especially since he was helpless to do anything for them at all, and he was thankful Lina filled up some of the empty space in their lives.

Now, sitting across from them, with only a few minutes left before the guard would take him away from the visiting room, there was one thing he hadn't told them that he desperately needed them to know.

"Mom, Dad," Andrew said, looking at them through the bulletproof glass. "I love you."

Both of his parents cried.

Chapter 12

The Washington State Department of Corrections (DOC) was in a quandary. And as a minor convicted as an adult, Andrew was right in the middle of it. The law didn't allow the DOC to put Andrew in the same cell as the adults, because he was a minor. But they couldn't put him in with the minors, because he was charged as an adult. They also couldn't just leave him in solitary confinement without a disciplinary reason. So for weeks Andrew waited in his cell in Shelton for them to figure out what to do with him.

Finally, in July, Andrew learned that they had apparently found some kind of loophole. They were going to transfer him to Green Hill, a maximum-security juvenile institution, and place him in permanent administrative segregation in the Intensive Management Unit. It was a legal solution for the Department of Corrections, but to Andrew, it was just more solitary confinement under a fancier name, only this time at a juvenile facility, where he would stay until he turned 18 and was old enough to be placed in an adult institution.

Andrew rode a prison bus from Shelton to his new place of incarceration in the Fir Cottage at Green Hill. It sounded nice when they told him where he was going. When Andrew arrived, however, he discovered that the warm and fuzzy name was really the only thing nice about it. Green Hill was a maximum-security juvenile detention center, and Fir Cottage was just the name of his unit. Fir Cottage contained 16 individual rooms that were mainly used for disciplinary reasons when one of the juveniles caused trouble and was sent to solitary. There were three other teenagers who were in the same situation as Andrew, convicted as adults but too young for adult prison, who occupied rooms in the unit. Andrew had barely had time to adjust to his new solitary suite when his new case manager, Frank O'Dell, introduced himself.

During his nine months in the prison system, Andrew had encountered a lot of prison staff members. Most of them, it seemed, were just there to punch in, put some mind-numbing hours on the clock babysitting criminals, and then punch out to go home without really having ever been there. Some of the prison staff were decent individuals, of course, but a lot of them were small-minded people with superiority complexes who seemed to enjoy provoking, belittling, or exploiting the inmates.

Frank, however, was different. He was genuinely present, and Andrew could tell he actually wanted to be there. He treated Andrew like a human being, like a sentient person actually capable of intelligent thought. He didn't pull any punches, though. When he had something to say, he said it. He was laid-back on the outside, with a no-nonsense core. Andrew liked him immediately.

They met formally once a week, but sometimes Frank would come and play card games with him or bring him books to read. In addition to reading his Bible, Andrew read everything else he could get his hands on—he even devoured books about fish or cars or state history. Frank seemed to find Andrew's voracious reading habits fascinating and amusing, and he liked to find new material for Andrew to read.

Frank was also his counselor, and Andrew found him easy to talk to. Frank asked about his family, his crimes, what behaviors led to his crimes, what things in his life were working, what things weren't working, and what he could do to change those things.

"Look," Frank said one day as they sat together during one of their sessions. "I don't want to dwell on negativity. Yeah, your crimes occurred. Everybody has a closet. Everybody does stuff they shouldn't do. Some get caught; some don't. Fortunately, you got caught."

"Did you say 'fortunately'?" Andrew asked.

"Yes," Frank said. "Fortunately. Because what you were doing with the drugs and alcohol and the stealing, your personality and demeanor, was going to get you killed—or you would have killed someone. Fortunately you got caught, and that stopped that behavior. It made you recognize you were going down a path of destruction. For whatever reason—whether you were mad at your parents, whether you were angry about your brother's death—it happened. Now you have an opportunity to better yourself. So where are we going to go from here?"

Andrew was quiet as he listened. He liked to process things in his mind. He didn't always say very much, and he could tell Frank wondered what he was thinking, but sometimes Andrew needed to think without talking.

Frank studied him. "Let me tell you something. I've got a caseload history that could sink a barge," he said. "I've seen everything. Young guys get sent here, and they come in with a bunch of swagger, you know, with something to prove. They don't want to listen, they get in fights, they cause trouble."

Frank sat back in his chair. "But you . . . you stick out like a sore thumb, Andrew. And I mean that in a good way. You're looking at a long time behind bars, and I want you to try to see it as an opportunity."

"An opportunity?" Andrew finally said. "How is living in a cage for the next 12 years an opportunity?"

Frank nodded thoughtfully. "Andrew, almost all these other guys who are in the system for a short period of time—get out and immediately go back to where they came from—usually the same broken homes in the same neighborhood, with the same friends and same bad habits. But you— you can use the time you spend in incarceration to reinvent yourself. I think prison is actually going to give you a chance if you'll take it. Get your education, find your faith, obtain a skill."

Andrew processed the idea of reinvention. He'd already changed since he began reading his Bible. What if, as Frank said, this *was* an opportunity?

Frank continued. "Do you know how lucky you are? Of all the places they could have sent you, you were brought here to Green Hill. This is the only place you can pursue your high school diploma, if you want it. Dave Rust from the school will work with you on it if you choose. Yeah, you may be incarcerated, but that doesn't mean you can't do things. It doesn't mean you can't educate yourself. Doesn't mean you can't better yourself as a human being. You can achieve positive things."

By the time Dave from Green Hill School came by to talk with him about school opportunities, Andrew had already decided he wanted to work toward his high school diploma. Before long, Dave had deposited a huge stack of books and papers in Andrew's cell with assignments and instructions.

As soon as Dave left, Andrew opened up the books and started working on his assignments. Time passed by much more quickly when his mind was busy, and before he knew it, he had completed all of the work Dave had given him.

The next morning Andrew got up, drank a lot of water, and did push-ups. Though he'd been exercising to stay healthy, he now had another motivation to work out. On his classification papers the officials had noted that he looked "weak and frail."

Weak and frail? Andrew thought. *I'll fix that.*

He'd been doing push-ups every day since then, and he was getting stronger. Some days when he had nothing else to do, he would pump out a few hundred push-ups. He had reclined on his mattress and was reading his Bible when Dave came by to check on him.

"How are you doing with your schoolwork, Andrew?" he asked.

Andrew sat up and picked up the entire stack of books and papers. "Here you go," he said.

Dave looked disappointed. He sighed. "Andrew, I can't make you get your education. It's up to you, but right now you have the chance to get your high school diploma. I hate to see you waste it. Don't you want the opportunity?"

No," Andrew said, hurrying to explain. "I mean yes. I mean, I did it already. I finished all the assignments you brought me. See?" he pointed to the finished work.

Dave looked confused as he looked in the direction Andrew pointed. "You finished . . . *all* of it? All of those assignments are done?"

Andrew nodded. "Yeah, I did them yesterday."

A strange look came over Dave's face as he slowly realized what Andrew had said was true. He grinned in amazement. "Andrew, that's awesome. Let's keep up the momentum. I'll bring you more."

Not only did Andrew finish the assignments quickly, but he also aced them. Dave seemed excited about Andrew's progress. With no distractions, Andrew sat for hours reading his textbooks and completing his assignments until his wrist ached. It felt good to stop for a minute and stretch, but it felt even better to be doing something productive.

Frank was right, Andrew thought. *If they had sent me somewhere else instead of Green Hill, I wouldn't be earning my way toward a high school diploma.* He had read a lot of stories in the Bible about how God guided people, such as Daniel, through their circumstances, and he recognized that his transfer to Green Hill wasn't a coincidence. It was a present from God, and he wasn't going to take this opportunity for granted.

The weeks stretched on endlessly. Andrew's seventeenth birthday came and went. Once in a while they would handcuff Andrew and escort him to and from the school in shackles so he could complete certain projects. During those times Andrew sucked as much fresh air into his lungs as he could, grateful to be outside, even for a few moments.

One day Frank came by his cell. "Andrew, I feel bad. You're stuck here by yourself. Most kids come in here to be disciplined for behavior, but you live here. Except when we escort you to the school, you never get to go outside. You never get to swim in the pool or do any of the other activities that the other juveniles are allowed to do."

"Well, thank you very much for making me feel worse than I did 30 seconds ago," Andrew said jokingly. "I'll just sit here and ponder that."

Frank smiled. "I'm not finished. We want to do something for you, something special to try to make up for your having to be alone all the time. We got permission to give you this." Frank handed a black box to Andrew.

"This is for me?" Andrew asked, turning the box over as excitement built in his chest.

"Yep," Frank said. "It's a little radio, and it's yours."

"Thank you!" Andrew said, barely able to choke out the words. He resisted the urge to do a happy dance in front of Frank. He couldn't wait to turn the radio on and explore the local stations. The thought of being able to listen to music or hear news or conversations on talk radio—any kind of connection to the outside world—made Andrew feel like an excited little kid.

One Sunday evening Andrew held his radio up to the window and slowly twisted the tuning knob. In between each station white fuzz crackled and merged different stations into an annoying hybrid of sounds. Music. News. More music. Different music. Andrew wasn't in the mood for any of the stations he heard. He turned the radio antenna slightly and twisted the tuning knob a little farther until a voice came out of the speaker.

"Just before our break we had a question from a caller in Florida regarding what happens when people die," the voice said.

Andrew paused. *What in the world? What is this?*

"Caller, are you still with us?"

"Yes," the caller said.

"All right. Now your question was connected with Daniel 12:2. It says, 'Many of those who sleep in the dust of the earth shall awake, some to everlasting life, some to shame and everlasting contempt.'"

Andrew had just read the book of Daniel a few months ago. He recognized that verse. He scooted back on his bed to listen.

"This is a reference that Jesus makes when He says, 'The hour is coming in which all who are in the graves will hear His voice and come forth—those who have done good, to the resurrection of life, and those who have done evil, to the resurrection of condemnation' [John 5:28, 29, NKJV]."

"The Bible tells us there are two resurrections that take place, but they do not take place until Jesus comes," the voice continued. "Caller, if you, and anyone else listening, look in the New Testament in 1 Thessalonians 4, it tells us—especially if you start reading at verse 13—that Christians do not need to sorrow as others that have no hope regarding those who have died."

Andrew quickly reached for his Bible and turned pages as quickly as he could to find the book in the Bible called 1 Thessalonians.

"'For if we believe that Jesus died and rose again, even so God will bring with Him those who sleep in Jesus.' Now here's the part we don't want to miss," the voice said. "'The Lord Himself will descend from heaven with a shout, with the voice of an archangel, and with the trumpet of God. And the dead in Christ will rise first.' The resurrection of the dead in Christ is first, but when does it happen? When Jesus comes!"

This guy really knows the Bible, Andrew thought.

The voice continued on. "And then you read again in the Gospel of John it says, 'the resurrection in the last day.' It's very clear from the Bible that people are not resurrected with their glorified bodies until Jesus comes. If a saved individual dies, they rest in their dusty grave until Jesus comes, and their next conscious thought is of the Lord."

Andrew couldn't look the verses up fast enough, and he scribbled them down so he wouldn't miss any of them. That way he could look them up at his own pace.

"Just as when King David died, the Bible tells us in Acts 2 that David is dead and buried and not yet ascended to heaven. Although David died 3,000 years ago, for him it will seem like three seconds and he's resurrected when Jesus comes. The dead in Christ rise at that point. We have a study guide that deals specifically with this, and we will send it to you or anyone else for free, if you have more questions. I want to remind our listeners that the reason we keep providing the study guides is that the *Bible Answers Live* program is a catalyst to touch on many subjects, but for thorough study, we'd have to take the whole broadcast just on one question."

So that's what this is: Bible Answers Live, Andrew thought.

Andrew remembered the man who had grabbed him at Chris's funeral and told him that Chris was looking down on him from heaven. Now as Andrew looked up the verses the voice on the radio mentioned, he could see that Chris wasn't in heaven, or anyplace else. He was in his grave at the cemetery. *I'm glad he's not up in heaven looking down and watching my parents cry over him every day,* Andrew thought. *But Chris didn't even really have the chance to know God, other than going to church once in a while when we were kids. Will he even be saved?*

"The study guides give us a chance to put more information and more scriptures in your hands in a very colorful and attractive format," the voice was saying. "There are color illustrations, thought-provoking questions, lots of Bible references, and other illustrations, so please take advantage of these study guides. They're free!"

Andrew decided he would ask Frank or Dave to help him order the Bible study guides. Every answer he found from the Bible seemed to come attached to more questions, and he wanted to know the truth. He learned that the voice belonged to Pastor Doug Batchelor from Amazing Facts, and the program aired every Sunday night.

Andrew lay down on his bed with his Bible on his chest and looked up at the ceiling, thinking about Chris. Maybe God had found a way—a secret passage into Chris's life that nobody knew about—and Chris would be resurrected from his grave someday to meet Jesus. He hoped so.

Andrew thought of a verse in the book of Psalms: Psalm 25:7: "Forgive the rebellious sins of my youth; look instead through the eyes of your unfailing love, for you are merciful, O Lord."

Andrew began to pray. *God, if You can find a way to be merciful to me in spite of everything I've done, I know You can find a way to be merciful to my brother, even though he's gone.* He thought about his mom and dad, and about the bronze gravestone with Chris's name on it marking his resting place at Fir Lane Memorial Park. *God, please don't forget about Chris.*

Taking a deep breath, Andrew turned over and closed his eyes.

Chapter 13

"D addy, drive faster!" Andrew called from the back seat. He could barely see the tops of the trees blurring past the window. "Are we almost there?"

"One more block," his dad said. "Can you hold it just a little longer until I get the door unlocked and you can get to the bathroom?"

Andrew bounced up and down in his seat. Nope. He'd had a whole cup of soda pop at the burger place. "I can't wait!" he said frantically.

"Honey, if you can't wait until Daddy unlocks the door, go ahead and run around to the side of the house where the trees are and go there," his mom said. "Make sure the neighbors don't see you."

The car pulled into the driveway, and Andrew fought with his seat belt. Finally it unfastened, and he pulled with all his might on the door handle. He jumped out of the car and ran across the lawn to the side of the house by the big bushes. As he came closer, he noticed something that made him stop in his tracks. Broken glass. Everywhere. Shards of glass crunched under his feet. He looked up at the window. It was gone, except for a few jagged edges.

"Daddy!" Andrew yelled, forgetting everything else and nearly tripping over himself as he ran back to the car. He knew something was terribly wrong, and he started to cry. Did a bad person break the window to get inside? "Daddy! Daddy!"

Andrew woke up suddenly. It took a few minutes for him to adjust to his surroundings and realize where he was. Gloomy early-morning light filled his cell with gray shadows, and Andrew pulled his blanket up over his head.

The dream was a memory that replayed itself inside his mind during the night hours when he least expected it. It always arrived in Technicolor, though darkened around the edges by a sense of foreboding, a sense of danger that he couldn't eliminate no matter how many times he reassured himself upon awakening that it was over and that he was safe.

The event had occurred during the summer just before he turned 8 years old. After John's funeral, Andrew's parents had taken him and Chris to the lake house for a few days. Chris was too young to understand anything about what had happened to John at the time, and all Andrew had understood about death was that his older brother wouldn't be living with them anymore. His little wheelchair was gone, along with his special bed.

At the lake house his parents were sad rag dolls, quietly baiting the hooks on the boys' fishing poles as Chris and Andrew had cast the lines into the water again and again, unfettered by the deep sense of grief that numbed their parents. Their mom and dad had probably hoped that a few days in the fresh air with the lake water lapping gently up against the dock would soothe the edges of their sadness. Looking back, Andrew wasn't sure if it had helped them or not. All he knew was that when they had gotten home, they had had another sad surprise waiting for them. Someone had broken into their home and burglarized it.

Even now, as Andrew lay in bed, the emotions poured through him, just as intensely as they had when he was 7. The fear of wondering if someone was still hiding inside their house, waiting to hurt them. The sense of loss as his parents made discoveries of missing heirloom jewelry, a gun collection unaccounted for, and treasured items smashed to pieces on the floor. The hurt of knowing that someone had deeply violated them, their home, and their sense of security   someone who likely didn't even know them, but had taught them a painful lesson in what hatred felt like. He wondered who would have done that to them.

And then, in the predawn light, like a cold splash of water on his face, Andrew understood. He squeezed his eyes shut. He remembered the newspaper article his parents had told him about not long after he'd been arrested. It mentioned the last house they'd robbed, on 64th Street, the one with the kids' toys in the yard. Inside, the article had said, a 5-year-old girl watched as the four robbers in scary masks held her mother at gunpoint and punched her 14-year-old brother as he slept. When the little girl had cried out, they had told her to shut up.

She must have been so terrified, Andrew thought, his stomach hurting as badly as if someone had punched it. She probably hovered, scared and crying, in the bathroom with her mother and brother while her mother counted to 100 and prayed that the robbers wouldn't come back and hurt them anymore. And all the while Andrew was sitting outside in the getaway car, making it all possible with no guilt or remorse, indifferent to the horrific crimes that were happening inside.

The realization was almost more than Andrew could stand. He knew what it felt like to be violated and hurt, and he'd done even worse to someone else. A little kid no less. He wondered if that 5-year-old girl still had nightmares too.

Andrew picked up his Bible to look for a verse he remembered reading in the book of Matthew. He turned pages for a minute, trying to find the right place. He found the verse he was looking for—Matthew 18:10: "Beware that you don't despise a single one of these little ones. For I tell you that in heaven their angels are always in the presence of my heavenly Father."

Andrew thought of the kids' angels going to the throne of God to report the story of what had happened that night to that little girl and her brother. *Oh, God, I'm so sorry,* Andrew prayed. *Forgive me.* Each time he gained a deeper understanding of the hurt he had caused, he prayed for an even deeper level of forgiveness.

I've got to do something, Andrew thought. He sat up in bed and dropped his feet over the edge onto the cold floor. *I've got to tell them I'm sorry.*

He reached for his pencil and paper as his mind started turning. He would write letters to every single one of his victims. He would tell them how sorry he was.

He started writing slowly at first, trying to find the right words. Soon it all began pouring out onto the page—a genuine expression of regret and sorrow. Even as he wrote the letters, he knew they might not make a difference. His victims might never receive them. Or they might receive them and not believe he was sincere; they might even choose to hate him for what he had done regardless of his regret.

He wrote to every victim anyway.

As Andrew continued to study his Bible, he came across a story in the book of Joshua that really bothered him. It was the story of Achan.

At God's command, Joshua was leading the Israelites on a conquest of Canaan. With God helping them, they overthrew city after city, including Jericho. Before they took Jericho, however, Joshua had warned the men not to take any of the gold or silver plunder for themselves or they would bring trouble on the whole group.

Everyone did as they were told, except for one man. Achan stole a beautiful robe, a wedge of gold, and some silver and hid the items under his tent. Not knowing this, Joshua sent the Israelite soldiers to attack the next town, Ai, but Ai fought back, and not only did Joshua lose the battle but many men died. In the end Achan finally confessed to what he'd done, and he and his entire family were put to death. After that, the Israelites conquered Ai.

Wow, Andrew thought. *Achan was a thief too. And the stolen stuff he hid under his tent caused a curse on him, his family, and the entire Israelite group.*

Andrew began sifting through his parents' house in his mind. He had hidden, all throughout their home, stolen items that his parents didn't know about. *Are those things a curse to my family?* Andrew wondered. More than anything, he wanted to get out of prison and get rid of every single stolen item. He didn't want any remnants of his life before God left over, especially not things he had stolen. He stared through his bars, knowing it was futile to wish.

God, please let me get out of here. I want to get rid of all that stuff hidden in my parents' house. I want to be totally transparent, with nothing to hide. Andrew shook his head and buried it in his hands. *But if You don't let me leave here early, I promise that 12 years from now when I get out that will be the first thing I do.*

Months passed. Every day Andrew worked on his homework assignments and studied his Bible with the Amazing Facts Bible study guides. On Sunday evenings he tuned in to KACS 90.5 FM in Chehalis, Washington, to listen to Doug Batchelor on *Bible Answers Live.* Andrew's brain felt as if it were stretching his skull as he absorbed new information about Jesus' second coming, where the dead go when they die, and the truth about the seventh-day Sabbath. Everything he heard on the radio, and everything written in the Bible study guides, he compared with the verses in the Bible. It all seemed to match up perfectly.

Andrew's routines were simple, but from sunset on Friday until sunset on Saturday he took a break from his schoolwork for Sabbath. The 24-hour rest from his assignments and his focus on God during those special hours seemed to recalibrate him, physically and spiritually. It was a weekly reminder that he could never work hard enough to earn forgiveness or overcome sin. It was God's job, with Andrew's permission, to confront him, to forgive him, and to reinvent him, just as He had with the people Andrew was reading about in the Bible.

One of the stories Andrew found in the Bible was about a guy named Saul, who had committed himself to the bloody task of killing Christians. One day he was on his way to a town named Damascus, where he'd planned another attack to wipe out the spread of the Christian doctrines. Suddenly a bright light from heaven shone down on him, and Saul was blinded. Jesus spoke to him and asked Saul to stop persecuting Him and His followers. Saul was blind for three days until God sent another man named Ananias to lay hands on Saul so he'd be able to see again. After that, Ananias gave Saul, whose name was changed to Paul, instructions on what to do next. Andrew had read it in Acts 22:16, and the words swirled around in his head again and again. It seemed like a message for him, too: "And now, why delay? Get up and be baptized, and have your sins washed away, calling on the name of the Lord."

It wasn't the first time Andrew had read about someone making the decision to follow God and then getting baptized. Even Jesus was baptized, and He had never sinned!

I want to be baptized, Andrew thought. *I've decided to live my life with God, and now I need to be baptized.* He looked around his cell, and his heart sank a little. How could he possibly be baptized? Other than his one hour of recreation, he was stuck in this cell.

Andrew had met the facility chaplain, Elaine Parker, a few times, although he had never studied the Bible with her. She had been coming to counsel with him, and the next time she came to visit he told her about his desire to be baptized. "I guess it's probably not possible," he said.

Pastor Elaine smiled. "If you want to be baptized, we'll figure out a way. Let me work on that."

In April 1997 Andrew completed his high school studies. Green Hill School held a small commencement ceremony, and Andrew's parents and grandparents were able to come see him receive his diploma. He even wore a cap and gown. Andrew Michell, the kid who got kicked out of every school he'd ever attended, graduated with a high school diploma a year earlier than he would have if he'd stayed in high school—and with a 3.7 grade point average. It felt good to see his parents and grandparents proud of him. Frank had reminded him again and again how fortunate he was to have a family who supported him. A lot of the juveniles at Green Hill never received any letters or visits from anyone, and Andrew's parents had continued to visit him as often as they could.

While Andrew enjoyed seeing his parents and appreciated their support, their visits often left him feeling melancholy. It was difficult to explain; his parents lived in a different world—a world that, to Andrew, was becoming a vague memory. After a year and a half in the prison system, his knowledge of the outside world and the way it worked was gradually being erased. On the flip side, no matter how he explained it, there was no way his parents could comprehend the depth of his life in solitary confinement.

The transitions into and out of visits were especially hard. He'd leave his cell to play Scrabble with his parents or sit in the visiting area challenging each other's vocabulary with the dictionary and eating food from the vending machine. But at the end of their time together Andrew had to watch his parents walk out first before he was led back to his cell. After saying goodbye, Andrew always felt emotionally and physically exhausted, and would usually collapse on his bed for the rest of the day. Those times right after the visits, he didn't even feel like talking to Frank. It was difficult, but Andrew knew he had to deal with it. For the decade that stretched out in front of him, this was the way his life would be.

Twelve days after his high school graduation, two guards escorted Andrew from his cell to an old, dilapidated swimming pool on the grounds of Green Hill. Pastor Elaine had kept her promise to see that Andrew was baptized. He had been told it was quite an undertaking to meet security precautions for the event; but shackled, and with his hands cuffed to his waist, Andrew made his way down into the water to meet Pastor Elaine for his baptism. Aware that their charge was considered a high-risk DOC prisoner, guards watched his every move. Andrew couldn't help grinning. *I guess you can't be too sure of prisoners who want to be baptized,* he thought. In the swimming pool his chains were wet and heavy, but his heart was light as Pastor Elaine dipped him under the dirty water in the name of the Father, the Son, and the Holy Spirit.

Not long after his baptism Pastor Elaine dropped by to see how he was doing. They visited for a few minutes, and then she told him that another young man on a different floor was interested in learning about the Bible.

"Oh, man, I would love to talk to him," Andrew said. "I've learned so much since I've been studying my Bible. It would be so cool to be able to share it with him."

"It's too bad prisoners on different floors aren't allowed to communicate with each other," Pastor Elaine said. "He's actually in the cell directly above you."

After Pastor Elaine left, Andrew began thinking and praying. *There's got to be a way to talk to him,* Andrew thought. *God worked out a way for me to be baptized. Maybe He'll work out a way for me to talk to this guy and tell him my story. If God can make the sun stand still for Joshua in the Bible, He can get His message through the few inches of concrete between me and the kid upstairs.*

As Andrew's eighteenth birthday approached he began to wonder what would happen to him next and to which adult prison facility he'd be transferred. He had heard that there were a lot of educational opportunities at McNeil Island Corrections Center, and now that he had graduated from high school he wanted to continue to improve his mind through further education. He had already read everything he could get his hands on—at least twice—and was desperate for new knowledge. He decided to place a request for transfer to McNeil Island and wait to see what would happen.

To his surprise, Andrew learned that a television reporter wanted to interview him for a news segment they planned to air on KREM 2 News in Spokane called "Growing Up Behind Bars." Though he was nervous, Andrew agreed to do the interview.

They set him up in a chair across from the reporter, Dan Garrity, with the cameras filming him from the back so as not to reveal his identity. They told him they would refer to him as "Drew" for interview purposes.

Andrew answered questions about his crimes, about his fight experience in Pierce County Jail, and how he felt about his impending transfer to another adult facility.

Andrew swallowed. "Being a little kid and being weak, and being put in a place where everyone is an adult—it's scary," Andrew said honestly. "I'm scared. Scared of getting taken advantage of. Scared of getting beat up. Scared of getting raped."

When the reporter asked him about his experience during the last year and what it was like to grow up behind bars, Andrew was glad his identity was concealed. "It's so humiliating, so embarrassing . . . there's such a sense of loss that I've missed out on all the good times," he said.

After only a few minutes of answering questions, the interview was over, and Dan the reporter thanked him and left. Back in his cell, Andrew thought about all of the people who would watch the short segment on the news, maybe while relaxing on their couches after work, or while putting dinner on the table for their kids. Andrew knew his story would be of passing interest for a few minutes, and then the viewers' lives would go on and they would forget about him. It made Andrew feel desolate.

Part of his anxiety about the transition was the memory of his first taste of adult prison. He was pretty sure that that gang member's fist had left a permanent dent in at least one of his internal organs. Sure, he had been only 16 at the time of that encounter, but the prospect of trying to be a Christian in that environment and trying to stay out of trouble with the guards and the other inmates seemed like a catastrophe waiting to happen.

God, Andrew prayed. *I've been inside these four walls for almost two years. I've learned so much, and I've grown so much. I'm getting to know You. I'm changing. I'm not the same kid I was the night I was arrested. Please, please, if there's a way, get me out of here. I don't want to go to adult prison.* He figured God had probably heard that prayer from every prisoner who had ever faced the same four walls, but he prayed it anyway. The thought that God could intervene if He chose kept a tiny flame of hope flickering inside him.

One afternoon before recreation time, Andrew heard one of the prisoners in another cell talking. It sounded as though he was talking with someone, but Andrew could hear only his side of the conversation.

Who in the world is he talking to? Andrew wondered. *That guy is in solitary, too. There's nobody in there with him.*

It wasn't the first time he had heard distant, one-sided conversations such as this. Andrew wished he could see through the walls and figure out what the other prisoner was doing. *Maybe solitary confinement finally got to him, and he's out of his mind. Maybe he has an imaginary friend now,* Andrew thought.

The more Andrew listened, however, the more he was convinced that the prisoner was talking to another human. It was like listening to someone talk on a cell phone, except there were definitely no cell phones in Fir Cottage. During the next few days, when his recreation time came around and he could see into the other cells, Andrew carefully observed and listened to see if he could figure it out.

Finally, during one of his recreation periods, Andrew noticed something interesting. One of the prisoners took his plastic pillow, put it over the toilet seat, and began a pumping action. *He's pumping the water out of the toilet drain,* Andrew thought. *Why would he do that?*

When the water was apparently emptied from the toilet drain, the prisoner banged on the ceiling of his cell. Sitting next to the toilet, he began to talk. Andrew couldn't stop grinning as he caught on. The prisoner in the cell above must have done the same thing, and they were talking to each other through the empty toilet pipe. To the other guys, it was probably just an ingenious way to break the communication rules; to Andrew, it was a miracle.

Well, God, Andrew prayed, *looks like You've made a way for me to share You with the guy upstairs. Thank You for putting him in the cell directly above me.*

When Andrew got back to his cell, he put his plastic pillow over the toilet and began re-creating the same pumping motion he'd seen the other guy do. When the water was out of the toilet drain, he pounded on the ceiling, and then waited to see if the guy upstairs would know what to do. A couple of minutes later, as he put his ear next to the toilet, he heard a voice. It had worked. Andrew introduced himself through the empty plumbing, and the guy upstairs answered back.

Andrew sat next to his toilet talking through the pipes and answering the other guy's questions. It turned out that Pastor Elaine was right—he did want to know more about God and the Bible. Excited, Andrew shared everything with him, from why he was in prison to how he'd gotten his Bible, and the things he'd been learning from his studies. The other guy sounded excited too. To Andrew, it added a whole new meaning to the phrase "toilet training."

I guess God's ways are effective, regardless of how unconventional they are, Andrew laughed to himself.

In June, Andrew learned he was being transferred back to the temporary location at Washington Corrections Center (WCC) in Shelton, which had finally implemented a Youth Offender Program. With his eighteenth birthday only three months away, he felt it was the prison system's way of saying, "Happy Birthday. You're going to adult prison."

When Frank came by during their last visit, he looked at Andrew as if he wanted to hug him. There was emotion in his voice when he spoke. "You know, I'm looking at you, and I can't believe it. I read your file, and I think, *Is this really the same guy? Is this really the guy who was involved in strong-armed kidnappings and armed robberies?* It just doesn't seem possible."

Andrew smiled.

"Look," Frank said. "This transition into the main prison system is probably going to be the hardest thing in your life. You're going to be surrounded by criminals, by negativity, by dysfunctional relationships. You're going to be surrounded by big brother all the time, whether it's a camera or a guard, or the lieutenant in the gang. For the next 10 years you're going to have someone telling you what to do. You're going to have to adjust to that. Everybody has to play the game sometimes. Everybody has to pull a party line sometimes, but that doesn't mean you have to be stuck in that rut. You have so much potential to do better things. You're a quick learner. You're going to be OK."

Frank paused and cleared the emotion from his throat. "Someday you're going to get out of the system, Andrew. And when you do, I'm expecting big things from you."

Andrew's heart felt full of Frank's words. *Wow,* he thought. *This guy has huge expectations of me.* The more Andrew thought about Frank's words and their impact on him, the more convinced he was that God had impressed Frank to tell him those things. It was as though God was telling him not to waste a moment of his time in prison, because he was preparing Andrew for something in his future. *I wonder what "big things" I'm being prepared to do,* Andrew thought.

Soon after, they led Andrew out of the Green Hill juvenile facility and put him on the bus that would take him back to Shelton for processing. *Someday,* Andrew thought, *when I get out, I want to live such a positive life that no one would ever imagine I was once in prison.*

The bus hydraulics system let out a groan, and Andrew's head jerked with the forward motion as the bus lurched into gear and began to advance. Ready or not, the next phase of his life was about to begin.

Chapter 14

After nearly two years of solitary confinement, the noise level at the prison in Shelton seemed deafening, and the constant interaction with other inmates, particularly the guy who shared his cell, was overwhelming. Some of the things he heard and observed were strange to him, but although he'd had a lot of anxiety about being absorbed into the new prison scene, so far the guys at Shelton in the Youth Offender Program had been nice to him. They'd even warned him to watch his step, because the guards were typically harder on the young inmates. Granted, it was usually the young inmates that liked to cause trouble.

All the guys assumed he had just been transferred from the county jail and was therefore new to prison and unaware of the way the prison worked. When they found out he'd been in solitary confinement for almost two years, Andrew saw the shock written on their faces.

"What the ———" One of them swore, looking at him in amazement. "Two years in the hole?"

After that, Andrew noticed that some of the other prisoners regarded him as though he were a time bomb with only a few seconds left until detonation. "After two years in the hole, he's probably a little bit crazy," he overheard one prisoner say to another.

Andrew grinned to himself. One of the ways solitary confinement *had* affected him was that he'd become relatively comfortable alone in his thoughts, even when he was around other people. He figured that his tendency to be quiet and absorbed in his own thoughts also probably strengthened their suspicions about his mental stability.

Not long after Andrew had arrived at WCC, he was stretched out on the top bunk reading when he heard a voice shout, "Five-o!"

Five-o? Andrew thought. *What was that?*

A few seconds later another voice shouted, "Five-o!"

Finally, driven by curiosity, Andrew decided to find out what was going on. "What does 'five-o' mean?" Andrew asked his "cellie," Garcia.

Garcia laughed. "It's kind of an in-house warning system among the inmates. Guys are always smoking or doing other stuff that's going to get them an infraction penalty if they're caught, so when a guard comes by, someone will shout 'five-o' so everyone knows to put away their contraband."

"They don't get in trouble for yelling the warning?"

"Nah, you know, it's technically against the rules, but nobody ever gets a penalty for it. It's kind of a nonissue," Garcia said.

Andrew grinned at the idea of an in-house warning system. *I guess prison really does create a brotherhood of sorts,* Andrew thought. *With the amount of time we all spend together, how could it not?*

From the time he arrived at WCC, Andrew didn't hide the fact that he was a Christian. He still read his Bible and prayed, just as he had done at Green Hill. His habits quickly earned him a reputation among the other prisoners as a "holy man." They teased him about it good-naturedly, but Andrew didn't mind being the target of that kind of joke.

Every week, Andrew discovered, the prisoners were allowed to go watch a movie for two hours. Since not much happens in prison, movie night was a big event, and everyone always went; that is, everyone but Andrew. The other prisoners teased him about it.

"Oh, Andrew's such a holy man that he doesn't watch movies!" some of the inmates joked.

Andrew always laughed. The truth was that he didn't have anything against movies in general; he just craved those two hours of silence when everyone else was gone. All the cells were empty, and he could be alone to contemplate or read or pray. He had always been quiet, but it seemed as though the nearly two years alone had driven his thoughts deeper inside him, and he felt even more reserved than before. He observed a lot, but said little.

One night after everyone had come back from the movie, Andrew lay in bed trying to doze off. When he opened his eyes, he noticed furtive movements outside his cell. It was a guard sneaking past the cells obviously trying to catch someone in a prohibited act. Andrew grinned. "Five-o!" he yelled.

He had seen and heard guys yell the warning multiple times with no reaction from the guards, but tonight he had messed with the wrong guard. All Andrew could figure was he must have been in a bad mood. The guard flashed his light inside their cell and focused the beam, not on Andrew, but on Garcia.

"I heard you say that!" the guard shouted at Garcia. "You're going in the hole!"

Andrew waited for Garcia to tell on him, but there was silence from the bottom bunk. *He's going to go to the hole for me,* Andrew realized. *He's not even going to tell them it was me.*

Andrew knew there was no way he could let Garcia take the punishment for something he had done. He had broken the rules; it was his infraction.

"He didn't do it," Andrew said to the guard.

"What?" the guard shouted.

"It wasn't him. It was me. I was the one who said, 'Five-o.'"

A few minutes later the guards came to take Andrew to solitary confinement. They put handcuffs on his wrists and shackled him. They marched him roughly past the other cells and down into a long underground corridor through a tunnel to the hole.

Both guards pushed him along almost faster than he could walk, and one of them leaned toward Andrew's ear to speak. "Don't you say anything smart to me or you might accidentally fall on your face and break some teeth."

Really? Andrew thought. *I'm in a dark tunnel alone with two guards and my hands are chained to my waist. Why would I try to say anything at this point? They must think I'm really stupid.*

Andrew kept his lips closed and didn't say a word, even though the guards continued to try to provoke him. Finally they pushed him into a solitary cell and left him there for five days. Not only did he spend five long, lonely days in the hole; he now had a major infraction on his record—an infraction that would come back to haunt him later.

In October Andrew received some good news from his caseworker. His request for transfer had been approved, and he found himself on a barge in a chain bus being transported to McNeil Island Corrections Center. Stealing a few moments in the fresh air, Andrew breathed in the cool, saltwater smell of the Puget Sound and tried to see everything his eyes could possibly take in—including the jagged majesty of the white-dusted Olympic Mountains in the distance and the small boats that bounced freely on the choppy waves—before he had to once again breathe in the stale prison air and look at the sterile walls. McNeil Island was home to thousands of prisoners and a small residential community, but the majority of the island was a dedicated wildlife refuge, home to a diverse population of protected wildlife. Large birds coasted above the gray-blue waters, and seagulls hovered noisily above the barge.

Inside the sealed doors of the prison, Andrew silently walked with the guards to his new cellblock. Sometimes he wanted to be free so badly it hurt. When they walked him to his cell and shut the door, Andrew felt his soul wilt. *God, please let me go home early,* he thought.

"Hey, how's it going?"

Andrew looked up to see his new cellmate, a Black man with a wide smile. "Hey," Andrew said. "I'm Andrew."

"It's a pleasure, Andy. I'm Michael Jackson."

Andrew looked up in surprise. "You're . . . Michael Jackson?"

Michael laughed. "Yep. And it gets better. See this ugly White guy over here?" he pointed to the next cell over. The guy Michael pointed at waved to Andrew. "His name is Michael Jackson too. No fooling."

Andrew grinned. "Well, at least I won't have that many names to re-member," he laughed.

As soon as he could, Andrew registered for two classes through Pierce College for the fall and started working at the prison for 26 cents per hour. He spent a lot of time studying for his classes to make sure his grades stayed high. When he wasn't studying, working, or reading his Bible, Andrew enjoyed listening to Michael talk.

Michael, Andrew found out, had been in prison several times, and was happy to share his prison wisdom with him. Andrew couldn't imagine ever doing anything that would get him locked up again when he finally re-gained his freedom, but Michael had lost his freedom more than once be-cause of his inability to stay out of trouble.

"Andy, how old were you when you got locked up?" Michael asked Andrew one afternoon.

"Sixteen."

"You know," Michael said. "I watch you all the time. You're really smart. You're doing the right thing. You're not using drugs or getting in-volved in drama. You're going to school, and you're going to do good things when you get out. But," Michael said, shaking his finger, "when you got here, you were 16. In many ways you stopped developing at the age of 16. And when you get out of here, you're still, in some ways, going to be 16 years old. You will be 10 years behind everyone else your age. You have to be aware of that."

Andrew nodded, but he wasn't sure he completely understood. All he really knew at the ripe old age of 18 was prison life. He couldn't compare his life to the life of someone outside who was his age, because he had no idea what that life was like.

"Michael," Andrew asked, "why did you end up back in prison? It seems as though you would have done anything you could to stay on the outside. When I get out of here, I'm keeping my nose clean. There's no way I'm coming back. What happened with you?"

Michael thought for a moment. "You know, Andy, when I got out of prison the first time, it was like being a martian. I felt like I was a man from the moon, or like I was from Mars. I just had no idea what to do. I felt so out of harmony with the world."

Andrew listened, trying to process Michael's words.

"You'll hate it here," Michael said, "but you'll get comfortable here. You'll get used to the routines. You'll make friends. And then someday when you get what you wish for, when you get out of here, all that will go away. And you're going to miss it, because it's all you'll know."

Andrew shook his head. "No way. I'll never miss this place."

Michael chuckled. "We'll see."

Andrew didn't want to admit it, but Michael had touched on a nerve—a fear that had been occupying space in the back of his mind. This totally unnatural environment in prison had shaped his perspectives and his worldviews. *What if I get out of here and I can't function in the real world anymore? What if I never have a job? Or a wife? Or kids?*

With Andrew's new routine of work and school, his days seemed to repeat themselves again and again. Although he could watch TV and interact with other people—a definite improvement over solitary—he missed listening to Bible Answers Live on Sunday nights.

God, Andrew prayed, *it's harder here. I look around, and I see the most serious, degrading consequences of sin played out in the lives of the people I am around every day. Please help me. I need to know You more. I feel as if there are so many layers of truth to be discovered if You would only reveal them to me. Help me to be like Jesus—let people see Jesus in the cell with me.*

Sure, there were a lot of religious people in prison, but their version of Christianity was confusing to Andrew. *How can they say they are Christians,* Andrew wondered, *if they never pray, never study their Bibles, and aren't trying to be like Jesus?*

A few days later, however, Andrew overheard some of the guys talking about a church group that had started coming to McNeil on Friday nights.

"Are you serious?" Andrew asked. "A Bible study group?"

"Yeah," one of the guys said. "Apparently this guy by the name of Hurley wrote a letter to a church in Yelm and told them there was no one else of his denomination here, so they got some people together, and now they're meeting on Friday nights."

"Oh, that is fantastic!" Andrew said. "What church is it?"

"H'mmmm." The guy thought for a second. "I think they are coming from the Yelm Seventh-day Adventist Church."

Seventh-day Adventist? Andrew was amazed. *Like Doug Batchelor? I didn't know there were any Adventists in Washington State,* he thought. *I gotta go see this.*

The next Friday night Andrew took his Bible and went to meet the Adventists. That night Andrew sat in the back by himself so that he could listen and observe. It was a small group of people who seemed nice. They sang songs and conducted a Bible study. Sitting in the back, he knew he probably seemed unfriendly, but he wanted to be able to process everything he heard. He read every Bible text and made notes.

At the end of the study one of the members mentioned they'd be bringing DVDs of Doug Batchelor speaking. *No way!* Andrew thought. *So I don't have Sunday night* Bible Answers Live *on the radio anymore, but now I'll have Friday night Doug Batchelor sermons on DVD.*

Andrew couldn't wait for the next Friday night to arrive.

John, age 1½, Andrew age 4 months (December 1979)

Andrew, age 11 months (August 1980)

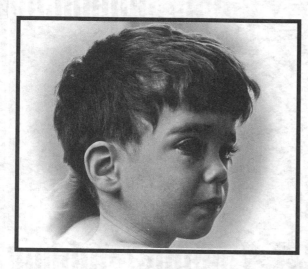

Andrew's older brother, John, age 5 (1983)

Andrew, age 6 (1985)

Andrew's younger brother, Chris, age 5 (November 1986)

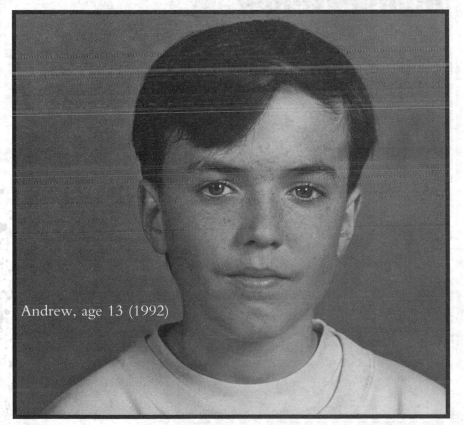

Andrew, age 13 (1992)

Andrew and his mom, Kathy, at his high school graduation at Green Hill in Chehalis, Washington (April 15, 1997)

At left, Andrew, age 18, at McNeil Island prison (1997)

Below, Andrew and his parents, Kathy and Don, in the McNeil Island Corrections Center visiting room (October 1998)

Speaking at McNeil Island
graduation (May–June 2007)

Bible camp for children, La Paz, Mexico (2007)

Refugee camp orphanage during Bible camp, Thailand-Burma border (2010)

Motivating youth to know God and read the Bible in Barquisimeto, Venezuela (2006-2007)

Teaching kids at a language center in Thailand (2009–2012)

"King of No" crown

With a little friend in Barquisimeto, Venezuela

With Eric (left) and a student while teaching Bible at Adventist school in Monteverde, Costa Rica (2009)

Andrew dressed as the apostle Paul, reciting the book of Philippians from memory (2010)

Andrew and Amazing Facts speaker, Doug Batchelor, Jakarta, Indonesia, ASI meeting (September 2011)

Chapter 15

In prison you know a man is dangerous if nobody talks about him. It was a survival tip that Andrew learned pretty quickly during his first year at McNeil. Nobody in prison would ever say anything—good or bad—about a dangerous man. Everyone knew that if word about something they'd said got around, someone could get killed. And if a guy's name never came up in conversation, it could mean only one thing.

Andrew noticed that Terry's name never came up in conversation. Terry was a big guy who worked on the educational floor where Andrew took classes. His arms were blue from a lifetime of prison tattoos, and he had a long ponytail that hung like a dead snake down his back. He had one eyebrow that seemed stuck over his eye, so he always had a crazy look on his face that intimidated everyone he came in contact with. It wasn't just the crazy eyebrow, however, that intimidated other inmates.

In the prison there was a quiet ripple in the underground conversation about how Terry had earned his formidable reputation. He'd gone to prison in 1978 for burglary; while in prison, he racked up more charges, including more than one attempted murder charge. He turned his original two or three years into more than 25 years. He was a problem child for the DOC, and they'd had to move him from prison to prison to try to keep him under control. He had previously been in Marion Prison, south of Chicago, where he'd lived a few cells down from the American mob boss John Gotti.

Andrew noticed that only a few select people were permitted inside Terry's inner circle—people Terry apparently knew well enough to trust. On his way to class Andrew began saying hello to Terry in passing. At first Terry regarded him suspiciously, but as the weeks passed, they began to exchange greetings. Andrew noticed that Terry watched him sometimes.

"Hey, Young Andy," Terry said one day as Andrew walked to class. "I walked by your cell at 4:30 this morning, and I saw you on your knees on the floor. What happened, man? Were you sick?"

"No, I was praying," Andrew said.

"Wow, really?" Terry said. "Praying, huh?"

Eventually Andrew and Terry began exercising together in the big yard and attending class together. It was an odd friendship—the kid with a good attitude who was always smiling, and the dangerous man with a legendary reputation for trouble who never smiled, not even when he laughed.

"Young Andy, why do I even spend time with you?" Terry asked one day. "We have nothing in common, but we hang out together all the time."

Andrew just smiled. He knew why. Terry didn't have to worry about him. He knew Andrew wasn't out to cause trouble or to backstab him. He could relax and be comfortable around Andrew, and in prison, where suspicion grows faster than mold on rotten tomatoes, that was a big thing.

"You're a good kid, Young Andy. You keep your nose out of trouble. I like that," Terry said.

Andrew was getting to know more people at the Friday night Bible studies also. He'd met Roger and Bev, who often led out in the meetings; Sheila, a little dark-haired woman with sparkling eyes and a huge personality; as well as others who came regularly to be part of the group. Over time the study group grew from four or five prisoners to a chapel full of guys who came regularly. Andrew knew that some of the guys came for reasons other than Bible study, but Andrew was there to learn everything he could.

During one of the meetings a leader read a quote from a book that especially caught Andrew's attention.

"'Our physical health is maintained by that which we eat.'" the leader read. "'If our appetites are not under the control of a sanctified mind, if we are not temperate in all our eating and drinking, we shall not be in a state of mental and physical soundness to study the Word.'"

I've got to find that book! Andrew thought. He couldn't wait for the service to end so he could ask about it.

"What was the name of that book, the one you quoted tonight?" Andrew asked.

"Let's see," the leader said. "That was *Counsels on Diet and Foods,* by Ellen White. The quote was on page 52."

"Oh, man," Andrew said. "Is there any way I can get a copy of that book? Ever since I read about Daniel's healthy diet in the Bible, I've been looking for a book about spirituality and healthy eating."

"They're pretty strict about not letting us bring items into the prison," the man said. "But let me see if I can get permission. If I can, I'll definitely bring one for you."

Lord, Andrew prayed, *please open the doors so the prison will let them bring that book to me. I want to take care of my body and my mind in a way that hon-ors You as my Creator.*

Andrew's prayer was answered the way he'd hoped. A few weeks later, before the Friday night meeting, the man put the book into Andrew's hands. "It's yours," he said.

In between his computer classes and work Andrew read the entire book and was fascinated by what he learned about the connection between what he ate and drank and his spiritual life. He decided to switch to a mostly vegetarian diet, and when he talked to the prison staff, they told him that the law mandated the prison to meet the dietary needs of the in-mates, whether those needs were for religious beliefs, allergies, or other health-related reasons.

During the following weeks Andrew felt really good. He was drinking a lot of water, exercising with Terry, and eating a healthier diet. His mind felt clear and sharp, and he did well in his classes. There was one other thing Andrew noticed: the nightmares he'd had since he was a kid began to dissipate, and he was sleeping better.

I wish I had done this years ago, Andrew thought. He'd had no idea eat-ing healthier foods and avoiding junk food would make a difference in so many areas of his life.

The end of December came around, and at the Friday night Bible study after Christmas Roger and Bev conducted the service. Bev began passing out little slips of paper to everyone in the group. "The new year is almost here," she said. "I want to challenge everyone to commit to read-ing the entire Bible in one year. Wouldn't it be great if by next December everyone here had read the entire Bible?"

Many of the group members signed their name on the slips of paper, and Bev smiled at Andrew as she offered a piece of paper to him. "Are you going to sign up, Andrew?"

Andrew already read the Bible every day, although not in a systematic way. But with Bev standing in front of him smiling, there was no way he could say no to this nice woman. "Sure, I'll do it," he said. He took the sign-up sheet and signed his name, "Andrew Michell." As Andrew fell into his normal daily routine, however, he forgot all about the slip of paper he'd signed.

A few mornings later, at 8:00, the bell rang as usual, and prisoners poured out of their cells to go about their daily routines. Andrew and Terry had already planned to exercise together, and when Andrew came around the corner, Terry waved. "Hey, Young Andy!" he called.

What's wrong with his face? Andrew wondered. *Something's different about it.*

It took him a few seconds to realize what was different about Terry.

He was trying to smile. Andrew knew that for Terry to show even that tiny bit of emotion—any kind of emotion—said a lot about their friendship. That attempted smile made Andrew's day.

I don't have to preach to people to show them Jesus, Andrew thought. *I just do my thing—smile and have a good attitude—and let them see what it looks like to have God in my life.*

★★★

It was mid-January 1998 before Andrew remembered his promise to read the whole Bible in a year. He read some, but not at a rate that would get him through all the books by the end of the year.

By May, Andrew was way behind in his reading. Summer quarter started, and he still had classes to study for in school. *I really should be reading my Bible more,* Andrew thought. He felt guilty.

September arrived. Andrew was irritated with himself. *Maybe Bev forgot, and maybe a few other people forgot, but God hasn't forgotten,* Andrew reminded himself. He had made a promise, and he was determined to keep it.

He began reading a few chapters every day, but by December he had read only one quarter of the way through his systematic study. *This is it,* Andrew thought. *If I don't read it, then I made a commitment and didn't follow through. I don't want to be a liar.*

Even though he had a massive credit load for fall quarter through Pierce College, Andrew created a schedule for himself that revolved around his Bible study. He woke up, ate breakfast, and then studied as much as he could in the morning; then, after work in the evening, he would read before dinner and after dinner until bedtime. Every free moment he had, he studied his Bible.

Cramming all of his Bible study into December turned out to be a strange sort of blessing. He read almost the entire Bible in one month, and it was the best month of his life as he immersed himself with Scripture and let it flood his mind. His outlook on life was better, and he felt even more at peace than he had before.

Andrew read a text, Hebrews 4:12, that seemed to sum up what he was experiencing during his month with the Bible: "For the word of God is full of living power. It is sharper than the sharpest knife, cutting deep into our innermost thoughts and desires. It exposes us for what we really are."

From that point on, he understood the importance of staying in the Bible, eating it, digesting it, and making it a significant part of his life. He couldn't live without it.

Chapter 16

Another new year arrived, and Andrew realized he'd been in prison for more than three years. Life in prison now stretched out for years behind him and years in front of him. It had become the only way of life Andrew could remember or imagine. During his time in prison Andrew noticed an odd catch-22 that affected not only him but also most of his fellow prisoners, and there wasn't much of anything they could do about it.

When Andrew was convicted of his crime, along with his sentencing he was also given an LFO—a Legal Financial Obligation. The court system expected him to pay financial restitution for his crimes. They had given him an LFO of $1800, and interest accrued on that amount at the rate of 12 percent until he could pay it off. Andrew realized that even though he was lucky enough to have a job, he was making only 26 cents per hour—not even enough to pay the interest that was accruing. He did some calculations in his head, and realized that by the time he got out of prison and could get a real job to pay his LFO, he would owe nearly three times his original amount.

At least I don't owe $30,000, like some of these guys, Andrew thought.

The part that was even harder was that the legal system looked down on prisoners who didn't pay off their LFOs and treated them as though they were trying to avoid responsibility.

But the truth is, they can't pay, Andrew thought. *I can't pay. What am I going to do?*

Andrew shared his frustration with his parents and asked them if they would be willing to pay his restitution for him, with the understanding that he would pay them back when he left prison. His mom and dad agreed. Andrew was grateful for his parents' help. Most of the other guys didn't have family or parents who would have done that, and Andrew recognized again how much of a blessing his parents were to him.

Andrew made almost $50 per month through his job, and he was careful what he spent it on. A lot of the guys bought tattoos or cigarettes or drugs with the money they made, but Andrew purchased granola bars, peanut butter, and little cans of tuna to keep in his locker so he would have something healthier to eat than the slop they served him from the cafeteria. He also used the money to purchase other items he needed or wanted.

One day as he munched on tuna right out of the can, Andrew pored over the most recent issue of the Tacoma *News Tribune*. He read several columns, and then he came to a news story that caught his attention. The story had happened in the little town of Orting, where his mother taught school.

A little boy had climbed the fence around his house and had accidentally fallen into a neighbor's yard. The neighbor had several large dogs that had attacked him and mauled his face and body. The boy had been rushed to the hospital, where the doctors had determined that he would need several surgeries. The article mentioned that the mangled boy's family was poor and didn't have the funds to pay for the hospital bills that were piling up, and implored readers to make a donation through Key Bank toward the boy's recovery.

Andrew looked down at his can of tuna and began to think. *I make only $50 a month, but do I really need that much? I have everything I need.*

The more he thought about it, the more he desperately wanted to contribute. For the first time in his life, Andrew sent a request to the accounting department to have a $10 check sent to the account for the boy. He knew that $10 was nothing when up against thousands of dollars of hospital bills, but after he had filled out the form and the $10 was sent, for the first time in his life he felt satisfied. He knew he had committed a selfless good deed for someone else. *Even if they use it to buy the kid a balloon or some stickers or something,* Andrew thought, *it's worth it.*

It felt so good to give that Andrew began to look for other causes to donate money to. He heard about some missionaries who were taking Bibles to China. For $5, they could purchase a number of Bibles. Andrew again went down to the accounting office and requested a check.

He might be in prison, but he could still make a difference. He believed in his heart that he *was* making a difference, and that gave him peace.

Winter quarter arrived, and Andrew again took a full course load. He liked to fill up his spare time with something productive, even if he was just casually reading a book for fun. The busier he was, the easier it was to stay out of the drama and trouble that seemed to lie in wait all around him. Now that he had settled in, he began to observe a contrast between the guys who were in prison for 15 or 20 years and the guys who were in for only a short period of time.

The guys who are spending most of their lives here don't want conflict, Andrew observed. He knew that the men who were in prison for most of their lives wouldn't tolerate an ongoing beef with another prisoner; they were more likely to deal with it by seriously hurting the person rather than argue with him. And while that's what they *would* do out of necessity, it wasn't what they *wanted* to do, so they stayed away from trouble as much as they could.

How are these guys avoiding conflict? How are they avoiding trouble? How can you be in prison for so many decades and somehow detach yourself in an environment where you really can't detach yourself? Andrew found it interesting, and he watched to see if he could figure out what made them succeed in prison.

One day, to feed his hunger for learning and to keep his thinking sharp, Andrew read a book called *The Complete Idiot's Guide to Motorcycles.* He knew he wouldn't be riding a motorcycle anytime soon, but he didn't care. It was still fun to read and learn. When he got to a section on target fixation, however, a new idea emerged that he began mulling over in his mind.

Target fixation is the concept that the motorcycle will tend to go in the direction the rider is looking. If the rider focuses on an obstacle, he may collide with it—even though he's trying to avoid it—because he's focused on it.

It made sense, not only in the world of motorcycles but also in prison. Andrew laid the book on his chest and remembered what he'd read in Proverbs 4:25-27: "Look straight ahead, and fix your eyes on what lies before you. Mark out a straight path for your feet; then stick to the path and stay safe. Don't get sidetracked; keep your feet from following evil."

That's it! Andrew thought. *That's how they do it.* He began to watch the lifers to see if his theory was correct, and it was. The guys who were in prison for a long time tended to avoid eye contact with other people. Looking at other people and their activities was like a magnet for trouble. It made sense, and Andrew began to apply it to the way he conducted himself.

Instead of walking around and looking at everything—especially at other people—he stayed focused. If he went to the library, he looked toward the library, and nowhere else. If he was headed to the gym, he looked at the gym, nowhere else. If he wanted to do well at his studies, he looked at his book and nowhere else. Andrew decided that, by far, the single most important helpful habit he acquired to deal with prison life was not to make eye contact with other people. If he saw problems, he didn't stare at them. He refused to look at the drama; instead, he looked toward where he wanted to go, because he knew his life would go the direction in which he was focused.

Andrew's life became even more interesting when he received a new cellmate named Winston. He was an old hippie, a vegan who ran a music store somewhere in the Olympia area but had a problem with drugs. He was a nice, easygoing guy, and Andrew liked him.

One night, however, not long after Winston came to share his cell, Andrew awoke from a deep sleep to the sound of screaming and crashing. He sat up in bed to see Winston thrashing around the cell, breaking everything and yelling at the top of his lungs.

"What are you *doing?*" Andrew said.

"Giant spiders, man," Winston yelled. "I'm killing the giant spiders! They're all over the place!"

Andrew looked around the room. "Winston, there are no giant spiders. Go back to sleep."

After a while Winston finally calmed down enough to go back to bed, and Andrew was relieved when he heard Winston's slow breathing and knew he was asleep. *That guy must have done a few too many drugs,* Andrew thought, shaking his head.

It wouldn't be the last time Winston commenced a valiant attack against the invisible giant spiders in their cell.

That summer Andrew started taking some welding classes as part of his Pierce College studies. He met a mean-looking guy with a soft heart whom everyone called "Junior," and they worked toward their welding certificate together.

"Your dad is so proud of you," Andrew's mom told him over the phone during one of their short conversations. "He's telling everybody about how you're learning to be a welder, and you're doing so well. He won't stop talking about you."

Andrew smiled at the thought of his dad being proud of him. He was glad he could make his dad happy after everything he'd put him through. Something lingered in Andrew's heart, however—a nagging doubt. He remembered conversations he'd had with his dad when he was still an angry, rebellious kid who wanted to hurt other people. His dad had tried so hard to get through to him, his only remaining son, and Andrew had spurned every attempt his dad had made to connect with him. Even though they had come a long way in their relationship during his incarceration, Andrew knew the bond still needed to be repaired, and it was not something he thought he could do fully during visiting hours.

One day while he was studying in his cell, Andrew was still thinking about the conversation with his mom and his relationship with his dad when suddenly Winston asked him a what-if question: "If you could have anything in the world, anything at all that you wanted, one wish and it would be granted to you, what would it be?"

Andrew put his book down. That was an easy one; he'd already thought about it many times. "There's nothing I want more than for my father to see me free," he said.

★★★

It was midmorning, around 9:00 or 10:00 a.m., when Andrew called home the next time. The phone was about 10 feet away from his cell, and Andrew was sitting in a chair with the receiver up to his ear. His dad had just had surgery, and Andrew wanted to find out how everything had gone in the operating room and how his dad was feeling.

Andrew dialed the number and waited while the collect call processed. He knew that on the other end there was a recorded voice warning his mom for the thousandth time that she was receiving a collect call from a prison inmate and that she should be cautious in accepting the call. When he finally got through, his mom handed the phone to his dad.

His dad was in a lot of pain, and Andrew could hear it in his voice over the phone as they talked. "When they opened me up, Andrew, they found that one of my lungs was full of cancer. They had to take it out. They took out one of my *lungs*. When I woke up, they told me some bad news," his dad said. After a painful pause, he continued. "Andrew, I have six months to live."

At that moment the scene before him burned itself into Andrew's memory. The chair underneath him. The cool, smooth phone receiver in his hand. The sound of his father's voice, telling him the one thing he didn't want to hear.

By the time Andrew hung up the phone, he was crying. He went back to his cell and knelt on the floor, crying and praying for his dad. He was thankful that Winston wasn't in the cell and that there was nobody else around. He knew at that moment that the thing he wanted most—for his dad to see him free—would never happen.

O God, Andrew prayed, *this is so painful. Please help me. Please help my mom and dad.*

Andrew cried until his tears ran dry. Then he lay down on his bed, exhausted from waves of impending loss. The pain worked its way deep into his core, and dark sadness began to seep into the cracks of his mind.

The consequences of your past life don't go away just because you meet Jesus, he told himself. *You've got to accept that. Those consequences of your actions are still going to follow you.*

Jesus had forgiven him. He was a Christian. But he was still in prison. He still had to deal with the result of his crimes—being in prison and separated from his family regardless of what was happening on the outside. It was hard being separated when his family was dealing with small issues; now he felt even more helpless as he thought of his father approaching death and the shadow of widowhood that was about to engulf his mother. His family was vulnerable, and there was nothing he could do. Once again, life was passing him by. Andrew was a distant, detached observer who couldn't even fully observe.

Andrew tried to call home as often as he could to stay in touch with his parents and learn how his father was doing. Knowing that his welding program was something that made his dad proud, Andrew took on all the welding classes he could handle, hoping to finish welding school so that his father could at least know he'd received his certificate.

Unfortunately, the downward spiral wasn't over. Andrew found out that the Department of Corrections had just finished building a new prison called Stafford Creek Correctional Center in Aberdeen, more than two hours away from McNeil Island toward the coast; they needed to fill beds at the new prison, and his name was on the list to be transferred.

No, Andrew thought. *This can't be happening to me right now.*

Andrew confided in one of his teachers about the transfer and his dad's health. "I can't go now," he said. "My father is dying. If I am transferred, he won't be able to come see me. It's too far away. He might die before I ever see him again."

His teacher helped Andrew put in a request for his transfer to be on hold so he could make a plea to stay at McNeil Island because of the hardship of his father's ailing health. As the final days of the fall quarter ebbed away, Andrew waited anxiously to find out if his request was approved. A few days later Andrew found out that because it had not been issued in time, his request was denied. He'd have to go.

At 4:00 a.m. a guard knocked on Andrew's cell door and woke him up. "Strip down, put on the orange suit, put your possessions in this box," he said. "You're going to Stafford."

Andrew slowly put each of his things in the box. Winston looked up at him from the bottom bunk. "I'm sorry, man," he said, knowing Andrew's situation. "Good luck to you."

Andrew nodded. "Thanks. You too."

A few minutes later the guards arrived and led Andrew away.

Chapter 17

If hell had an address, it would be 191 Constantine Way in Aberdeen, Washington. At least that's what Andrew thought as he looked around at his new surroundings.

Andrew's new home was cell 93 inside Stafford Creek Corrections Center, a cold and sterile place with a bed, a sink, and a toilet. It was not unlike his previous accommodations, except for one thing: there were no educational offerings at Stafford Creek, since it was brand-new, and so there was absolutely nothing to do. Because of his father's illness and the geographical distance, there was no way his dad could visit him, and the clock of his father's life was ticking away while Andrew sat in his cell alone. Boredom scratched around inside Andrew's mind like a mouse in a cage, and he wondered if he'd go crazy.

Forced idleness is far worse than forced labor, Andrew said, recalling a Napoleon Hill quote from one of the books he'd read as he alternated between sitting and pacing the floor.

Andrew was able to get a job working in the kitchen at the prison, which helped consume some of his time. And, happily, he'd discovered that his friend Brian had also been transferred from McNeil Island, and now lived a few cells down in 102. It seemed that no matter where Andrew was, Brian was always a few cells down the block. They'd even worked similar jobs. Brian knew Andrew's story, including how he'd met God in prison and how his life had changed. Brian had shared his story, too, about how he had become incarcerated.

Brian was from the Snohomish area, and had been in prison since he was 22. He'd gotten into a bar fight, stabbed the guy, and gotten 17 years behind bars. And now, because the DOC needed to fill beds in Aberdeen, they were neighbors once again.

From Stafford Creek, Andrew made an official request to be transferred back to McNeil. It was called a hardship transfer, and it was

Andrew's only hope to be close to his dad again. The weeks trickled on as Andrew waited for an answer.

The idle, lonely hours in his cell began to wear on Andrew. *I wish I had some good music to listen to,* Andrew thought. The more he thought about it, the more he craved it. Music could numb his senses and help him cope with his surroundings. It could overpower the stimuli that constantly reminded him of the awful consequences of his past decisions. Andrew began to think about the groups he'd loved before he got arrested, and decided to order a cassette tape by one of his favorite bands.

Danzig, Andrew knew, was a band that openly advertised their devotion to Satan and the underworld. Now that he was a Christian, he knew the lyrics would be in sharp contrast to his new belief system and relationship with God. *But I'm not going to listen to it for the message,* Andrew thought. *I'm just going to enjoy the music.*

When the package arrived, Andrew eagerly tore off the wrapping and looked at the cover art. It was creepier than he'd remembered. When he turned the music on, it felt like an old friend. The drums, the guitar licks, the voice—it was a powerful anesthetic.

As the lead voice growled an invitation to find hell with him, Andrew cringed at the lyrics. The words were distasteful, but the music felt so good coursing through his mind and body that he kept listening.

About an hour later Brian came by. "Hey, I heard you got a package," Brian said. "What came?"

"I ordered a tape by Danzig," Andrew answered.

Brian stared at him for several seconds. "Are you kidding me?" he said. "You sit there all morning reading your Bible and you just bought a tape by *Danzig?* How can you pray to God all day and at the same time listen to people who are blatant worshippers of Satan?"

Andrew didn't know what to say.

"You know what?" Brian continued. "The moment you began to listen to that music, all the little Holy Spirits in your cell ran away."

Brian wasn't the only one questioning Andrew's decision. *How can goodness be a partner with wickedness?* a voice inside Andrew's head said quietly. *How can light live with darkness?*

"You're right," Andrew said to Brian. "I'll get rid of it."

Andrew went back to his cell and cut the ribbon in the tape. He held the tape in one hand and put the end of the ribbon in the toilet. When he flushed, the ribbon whirred out of the tape in his hand and disappeared down the toilet. Andrew was mad at himself for wasting money on the tape in the first place.

Transitioning back to life with no music was hard. He liked his old hard rock favorites, but the lyrics were in opposition to his life with God. He didn't like the contemporary Christian music—either it seemed too antiquated, with all the "thees" and "thous," or it was just nicer lyrics on a background of music that resembled popular worldly music. He figured there was probably music out there that would satisfy his hunger; but in prison, his exposure to Christian music was limited. He'd have to keep looking.

Summer arrived, and with it, according to his case manager, Andrew's approval for transfer back to McNeil Island. Transfers happened on Monday at Stafford Creek, so every weekend for a couple of weeks Andrew waited in his cell, hoping that the next day would be the day. Finally, one Sunday night, a prison staff member came by his cell. "Pack up, Michell," he said. "Tomorrow morning it's the chain bus to McNeil."

It was a relief to be back at McNeil. Not only was Andrew finally able to see his dad again—who, by the grace of God, had outlived the doctor's six-months-to-live prognosis—but Andrew was also able to enroll in summer quarter at Pierce College and attend the Bible study group again. He picked up his welding job from before, so he was able to work as well.

From time to time Andrew would come across books about the Bible he'd use to guide him in his studies or to help him better understand biblical concepts. One of those books he found was called *Faith That Works,* by Morris Venden.

Each morning when he woke up, Andrew would reach over and turn on the little light clamped to his bedpost. He'd push it close to the wall so he wouldn't wake up the other prisoners. After praying, he would open his Bible and read, and then he'd also read from *Faith That Works.* He enjoyed it so much that he read the whole thing every day. It seemed as though the lessons he read were so important that he needed to remind himself of them every morning.

There were two basic concepts that intrigued him the most. The first concept was the importance of staying connected to Jesus; instead of fighting against sins, Andrew needed to fight to spend the time he needed with God, and not leave until he was filled with God's presence. The second concept was the idea that if he was connected to Jesus, he would "bear fruit"—he would live a life that looked like Jesus'. If he weren't connected to God, the "fruit" would be sin—whether it would be socially "acceptable" sin, such as cheating on taxes, or a socially "unacceptable" sin, such as murder. Ultimately, the consequences for both are the same. And, ironically, murderers are more likely to be keenly aware of their need and cry out to Jesus sooner.

Back at McNeil Island, something else about Andrew changed. Until now he'd been very quiet; he'd listen, but not talk—observe, but not participate. It was easier to get along with people that way. But the Bible story of Joseph inspired him.

Joseph was sold into slavery by his jealous older brothers, and was purchased by a powerful man in Egypt named Potiphar. Joseph did such a good job in his work as a slave that soon Potiphar had put him in charge of his whole household. Things were going well until Potiphar's wife tried to seduce Joseph, and he refused her. Furious, she claimed he had tried to rape her, and Joseph was thrown into prison, even though he was innocent of the charges. Eventually, through the amazing way God had prepared for him, Joseph was freed from prison and became second only to Pharoah in the land of Egypt.

It was what Joseph did while he was in prison, however, that inspired Andrew the most. He'd read in a book called *Patriarchs and Prophets*, by Ellen White, that Joseph didn't sit around in prison feeling sorry for himself; instead, he was able to forget his own sorrow by finding ways to lighten the sorrow of his fellow prisoners.

I can do that, Andrew decided.

Andrew could see, all around him, the greatest effects of sin on the men he lived with. He'd seen it in himself when he first met God and could finally see how dark his life was—it was horrifying to see how degraded people could become. The saddest thing was that none of these guys foresaw the consequences of that first wrong step. Most of them felt that they'd gone too far and that there was just no turning back. *This is what happens to people who don't know they have a Savior,* Andrew thought.

Andrew began showing a genuine interest and concern in the guys around him. He wanted to understand them and encourage them. He'd ask such questions as, "Why are you in prison? Where is your family? What about your education? Why is this your fifth time in prison?" The guys would open up to Andrew's honest face and share their stories with him.

One question Andrew asked everybody was "If you could go back to when you were a teenager, would you stay in school instead of getting involved with crime?" The answer was always emphatically the same from every person he asked: "Yes." Going to school, being able to spend time with their families, and living a humble life was much better than working a life of crime and paying for it behind bars.

Andrew began to develop incredible relationships with the other guys in prison through conversation and his sincere interest in them and their welfare. The minutes, hours, days, and years they spent together built bonds to such a degree that it seemed impossible to imagine that kind of friendship outside prison walls.

It was strange to know that several of the guys who were incarcerated with him were actually innocent of the crimes that sent them to prison. Billy was one of those guys.

"Andrew, this is my fourth time in prison," Billy told him one day while they were talking. "I've been in prison three times before, all of them for burglary. Every burglary was to steal things so I'd have money for drugs. But this time I'm innocent. I'm in prison, but I didn't do it."

"What happened?" Andrew asked.

"Well," Billy said, "I was walking along the street in a bad neighborhood. I found a wallet in front of a house. I picked it up and took it to the house. I knocked on the door, and the door swung open. Everything inside was a mess. At that moment the police pulled up."

Billy had been standing in front of a house that had just been burglarized, holding a stolen item, when the police responded to the call. They immediately arrested him and charged him with burglary.

"There was no sense in even trying to fight it," Billy told Andrew. "Because of my criminal history, no one would have believed me. I would have lost if I'd gone to trial. I told myself, 'I have a record. I can't fight this.' And I took the plea bargain, and here I am."

Andrew was surprised at how much he cared about the people around him. He'd gone from easily hurting other people without any remorse to now trying to find ways to listen to them, help them better themselves, and get to know the God who had changed him.

Every day Andrew's desire and resolve to live a disciplined, holy, God-seeking life became stronger. There was a lot going on around him in his environment that could easily distract him from fixing his eyes on his goal, but he made a conscious decision to fight against it. He was determined not to live a life of compromise, but to live a radical lifestyle that was completely, totally committed to God. Not halfhearted, but 100 percent. His desire was that by the time he was released, he'd be ready.

That October, with only four years left of his sentence, Andrew officially became a "short-timer." His new status made him eligible for work camp, and Andrew looked forward to the new opportunities on the island outside of the main prison.

Finally, when he was able to go to work camp, there would be no more waiting for bells to tell him what to do; he'd have much more freedom, he could walk around, and best of all, he could breathe fresh air.

Chapter 18

Unfortunately, Andrew's dreams of work camp at McNeil Island would have to wait. The Department of Corrections had other plans for him. Once again, they transferred him. Andrew spent three months at Olympic Corrections Center in Forks, Washington; then a week at Cedar Creek Corrections Center in Littlerock, Washington; and then, to his dismay, he was transferred back to Stafford Creek in Aberdeen.

While his father had held on to life longer than anyone had expected, his health was still declining, and it was a matter of time.

God, please don't let me be this far away when my father dies, Andrew prayed. *Please let me go back to McNeil Island.*

Once again Andrew put in a hardship transfer request and waited to see if it would be approved. Five long months later, in May, he was finally transferred back to McNeil Island. This time he was approved for work camp outside the main prison.

Andrew, by far, preferred work camp on the other side of the island to the main prison. The McNeil Island work camp was a big building with dorms. There were about 50 people in each dorm, and everyone got up at 7:00 a.m. to work. Although there were still tensions between prisoners, everyone tried to behave himself and not get into fights, because as "short-timers" they were nearing the end of their time in prison, and nobody wanted to stay longer than he had to. Some were even eligible for early release for good behavior. If he chose, each prisoner could save up his earnings to purchase a television or radio to put in the cubicle where he lived, ate, and slept. But the spaces were small, and the only thing that separated Andrew from the guy in the next cubicle was a piece of sheet metal. That's how Andrew met Andy.

Andrew's new home was cubicle J-27. Andy's was J-26. During the day Andy worked construction, and at night he worked in the education building as an assistant to the advisor. Andrew and Andy had classes together, and Andy was full of good ideas on what schools Andrew could transfer to when he was released, as well as what financial aid opportunities were available. Andrew came to value Andy's knowledge.

Andy's boss was Joseph Smyly, the advisor for the education department at the camp. Andrew recognized immediately that Mr. Smyly was a really neat guy, a quality person who was interested in helping the guys who wanted to learn more than just the regular classes that were offered. With Mr. Smyly's help, Andrew and Andy were able to take nonvocational classes— anthropology, psychology, history of the Middle East, and other classes—that would count toward an associate's degree. Mr. Smyly would stop at the Fort Steilacoom campus of Pierce College and pick up all the materials so they could study together and quiz each other. Andrew and Andy spent so much time studying together that they both received 4.0 grades in their classes.

Andrew went to work as a firefighter on McNeil Island. He discovered that inmates who were firefighters in the work camp often fought forest fires in Washington State, and inmates also handled much of the tree-planting efforts. Andrew quickly absorbed his firefighter technique training, as well as paramedic training.

During his time in the camp Andrew would call home once per week to talk to his parents and find out how his dad was doing. He could talk for only 20 minutes, and then the call would shut off. Andrew and his parents learned to time their goodbyes so the call wouldn't disconnect mid-conversation. Andrew's dad was alive, but gradually failing.

"I'm so tired of the prison," Andrew complained to his dad one day while they talked on the phone. "The food is gross, the guards can be complete jerks—they open up my mail and read through everything. I'm just sick of it."

His dad sounded irritated. "Well, why don't you just talk to the governor about all of this? Maybe he'll listen to you and let you out."

"Why would you say that, Dad? That's a totally bizarre thing to say. You know I can't talk to the governor." Then he paused and thought for a second. "Wait a minute," he said slowly. "That's actually a good idea."

His dad was obviously just reacting to Andrew's unusually pessimistic attitude, but unknowingly he had planted an idea in Andrew's mind. Andrew had heard the word "clemency" a few days before from another prisoner, but only in passing. Clemency meant the governor was able to effectively reduce a prisoner's punishment by allowing him to go free before the prisoner had served his full sentence. Receiving clemency, though, was about as feasible as winning the lottery or watching Santa Claus come down the chimney on Christmas Eve. It just wasn't going to happen. But when his dad mentioned the governor, Andrew thought more about the idea.

A few days later, while Andrew was walking around the track on the soccer field, a guy named Joseph started talking to him. "You know what?" Joseph said randomly. "You should apply for clemency." Joseph continued on talking about something else, but Andrew's attention span halted at those words.

That's three times in a matter of days, Andrew thought. *Before that, I've probably heard it only three times in the whole span I've spent in prison.* Andrew pondered this revelation. *God,* he prayed, *are You telling me to apply for clemency?*

Andrew let the idea percolate, but he didn't act on it. He wanted to think about it and pray about it. He wrote about his hopes for clemency in his journal, but he would rip up the pages and throw them away, afraid that his deepest desires could fall into the wrong hands and that people might think he was crazy for even thinking about it. He wrote other hopes and dreams in his journal too, such as his dream of someday going to Venezuela and other places in the world.

At work, earning 26 cents per hour was no great financial incentive, so Andrew looked at his job as a class and tried to learn everything he could from the experience. His work motto was "If you're not learnin' while you're earnin', then what are you doin'? You're wastin' time."

While working at the McNeil Island Fire Department—which was a real fire department, except the firefighters were inmates—Andrew studied all of the books he could about being a paramedic, responding to emergencies, tying ropes, and other techniques important to first responders.

One day at the fire station the fire chief walked up to Andrew. "Hey, Michell," he said. "I want you to be the engineer for the fire engine."

Andrew stopped what he was doing and looked up. "Chief, I don't think that's a good idea."

"Why not?"

"Well, number one, I was arrested at the age of 16, and I don't have much driving experience."

The chief shrugged and started to speak, but Andrew continued. "Number two, I was arrested as the getaway driver."

"So?" the chief asked.

"Well, as you can see," Andrew gestured, "We didn't *get away.* So you know my driving can't be that good. Number three, that's a $250,000 truck!"

The chief just laughed. "Michell, I really don't care. It's state property. You can learn how to drive on it."

And so it happened that Andrew learned how to drive a fire truck while he was in prison. During his time at the fire department he fought small fires, including one fire started on a mattress by a disgruntled inmate. He responded to medical calls for sick inmates; if the call were a serious one, such as a heart attack, he would help put the patient on the stretcher and take the inmate in a speedboat to meet the ambulance on the other shore. During his time firefighting he met a guy named Brandon, and they became friends.

On December 17 Andrew's parents celebrated their twenty-fifth wedding anniversary. At that time Andrew happened to be taking a class on parenting from the college, and the combination of the parenting coursework and his parents' celebration of their marriage resurrected an old fear, and Andrew felt a twinge of sadness. *Will I ever be a husband or a dad?* he wondered. *Or is that something else I forfeited with my choices when I was a stupid 16-year-old kid learning the hard way?*

After seven months of firefighting and paramedic training, Andrew decided he wanted to learn something new. He went down to the auto shop to talk to the supervisor.

"I want to learn how to work on cars," Andrew said.

The supervisor shook his head. "This is not a school. I am not going to hire you to learn. You need to already know how to work on cars before you can come here."

The next day Andrew went back to the supervisor. "I want to learn how to work on cars. I learn really quick."

The supervisor again denied Andrew's request. "No, you can't work here."

Day after day Andrew kept asking, until the supervisor finally made a deal with him: "If the other guys don't mind you asking questions all day, then you can come work down here."

All the guys knew Andrew, so they agreed to have him come work at the auto shop, even though he didn't know how to change the oil on a vehicle! Six months later, however, he was tearing apart engines and learning everything he could about cars.

After a few more months of work in the auto mechanics shop, Andrew decided to learn what he could about construction. He went to the construction crew, and they let him come work with them. Andrew came to work every day for 26 cents per hour, learning how to do plumbing, concrete, drywall, siding, roofing, painting, electrical, and other elements of construction. This was also the crew Andy worked on, since he had been a professional wood finisher on the street, and Andrew enjoyed coming to work every day with his buddy. John did drywall on the street and enjoyed teaching Andrew his craft. Another guy was a plumber who seemed to welcome Andrew's questions. They all liked Andrew's interest in learning, and they enjoyed teaching him. They were funny guys, too, and Andrew found himself laughing all day at their jokes.

Andrew felt so blessed to be able to be back at McNeil Island, learning a host of skills. Andrew recognized that he would probably never weld another piece of metal. He'd probably never do plumbing or program a computer in C++. But the reason he went to school was to keep his mind in a state of growth and learning. He knew his eventual transition from a life in prison to the outside world required an ability to think, learn, and adapt. While he doubted he would ever use the specific job skills or the information from the classes once he was on the "outside," he knew that learning was a good exercise for his mind and character.

May 13, 2003, was a rare sunny day for late spring in the Northwest. Andrew squinted into the sunlight and wiped his forehead with the back of his glove. They'd been on the construction site all morning, and as usual, the guys' comedic antics had kept him entertained while he worked. He loved being able to work outside, and the guys he worked with were hilarious.

About an hour before lunchtime the supervisor showed up on the site and called his name. "Michell!"

"Yeah?" Andrew said, taking his gloves off. "What's up?"

"They need to talk to you in the prison. You need to go back to the administration department. Come on, I'll take you."

Andrew's heart iced over, and the other guys fell silent as they looked at each other. They all knew there was only one reason anyone was ever asked to report to the administration department: bad news.

Chapter 19

The supervisor didn't say a word to Andrew as he drove him back to the prison, which only reconfirmed to Andrew that he could expect bad news when he arrived. Andrew rode silently alongside the supervisor as they headed toward the main prison. He suspected that the news was about his father, that maybe his father had taken a turn for the worse, but he didn't ask.

When Andrew arrived at the administration department, the lieutenant was waiting for him. "You need to call your mom," he said.

Andrew slowly dialed the numbers and waited. When he heard his mom's voice on the other end, he could tell she was crying, and Andrew held his breath, bracing for the news. "Andrew, your dad just passed away," she said.

Andrew stood there with the phone in his hand. His dad was gone. Just like that. No more seeing his dad's face in the visiting area. No more hearing his voice on the other end of the telephone line. No more seeing his handwriting on a letter in the mail. It was over. He wished he could reach through the line and hug his mom, but he couldn't. She was there, and her comfort was out of his reach; and he was here in prison, where he would have to process by himself the loss of the man he'd known all his life. When he hung up the phone, Andrew kept his emotions intact as much as he could until he was alone. Then he let it all go.

A few weeks later Andrew sat in his cubicle in personal clothing, fidgeting and waiting for the guard to arrive. As a minimum-security prisoner, he discovered he was allowed to leave McNeil Island for a short time to attend his father's memorial service. He would be accompanied to Fir Lane Memorial Park by a guard.

When the guard arrived, he put Andrew in the back of an old, decommissioned police car, and they crossed to the mainland on the ferry. The funeral home was not far away, but Andrew stared out the back window in awe. It seemed as if there were millions of people milling around on the streets, in and out of stores, and driving in cars. There was so much happening it was overwhelming to Andrew.

The memorial service was a nice tribute to his dad. One of his friends from the Yelm Seventh-day Adventist Church group sang a song while Andrew sat with his mom, his cousins, and other family members during the service and stared at the picture of his dad.

My mom and I are the only ones left, he thought sadly.

When the song was over, Andrew stood up to deliver the eulogy. As he stood before his family, neighbors, and friends, he spoke in a calm and thoughtful tone of voice. Although he was emotional drained, he had hope and a belief in God that strengthened him, and he prayed that that shone through him.

After the service ended, Andrew's mom whispered in his ear, "Everyone is proud of the positive changes they see in you, Andrew."

He smiled. It was a good feeling to know people were proud of him.

The memorial service ended all too soon and he was forced to say goodbye to his family and climb back in the car that would take him back to prison. It was so difficult to leave everyone behind and board the ferry. His life behind bars was still his reality.

Back at the work camp at McNeil Island, Andrew immersed himself in work and college classes. Summer faded into fall, and Andrew left the construction crew to work at the marine shop, where he learned how to perform mechanical maintenance and be a deckhand.

His friend Andy had reached the last six months of his sentence, and was now involved in a work release program that allowed him to work in Seattle. Andrew was happy to hear through the prison grapevine that Andy had gotten a well-paying job making $28 an hour doing woodwork. Within a few weeks Andrew discovered that Andy had proved his skills and impressed his superiors so much that he was now the leadman working on a yacht.

A couple months later Andrew stood on the deck of the ferry and breathed in the fresh open air. *I can't complain about my situation here,* he said to himself. *Where else do prisoners get to work on a boat and be outside going back and forth from the prison to the mainland? How many prisoners get to see fish and wildlife every day at work?* Andrew's last few years in prison, doing all of the jobs he'd been able to do, gave him a wealth of knowledge and experience. If he'd gone to school to learn all that, he couldn't even imagine how much that would have cost. And he got 26 cents per hour to boot.

After his father's death, Andrew thought a lot about clemency. It was a long shot—almost an impossibility—that anything would come of it even if he applied. He'd prayed about it, though, and was becoming increasingly convinced that God wanted him to apply. Privately, he began listing off the reasons he could qualify for clemency. He'd spent nearly eight years of his sentence in prison already. Besides his one infraction for yelling "Five-o," he didn't have any major infractions. He had demonstrated good behavior. He had taken every class offered by the prison, and he had achieved a couple hundred credits through Pierce College—he only needed 90 credits to graduate with a degree. Plus, he was pretty sure he could get a letter of recommendation, and he had his mom's support. The reasons seemed to pile up in his favor, so he decided to go for it.

Andrew talked with his mom, who arranged for an attorney from the outside to represent his interests at a clemency hearing in Olympia. She helped him compile the necessary paperwork. Now, he just needed a letter of recommendation. *Maybe Mr. Smyly would do it,* Andrew thought.

After work, Andrew walked into Mr. Smyly's office. Mr. Smyly looked up. "Hey, Andrew."

"I have a favor to ask," Andrew said. "Would you write a letter of recommendation for me? I'm going to apply for clemency."

Mr. Smyly smiled. "I'll do one better than that—I'll testify for you."

Andrew grinned. He couldn't believe it. It was more than he could have asked for. He knew Mr. Smyly was a busy man, and he already went above and beyond his regular duties as education advisor to bring Andrew the learning materials he needed for his studies, and now he was going to drive to Olympia on his own time to testify on Andrew's behalf before the clemency board. "Thank you," Andrew managed.

Andrew's case was scheduled to appear before the clemency board on December 19. In the meantime, Andrew began to feel a strange peace about him. He knew that God had led him to apply for clemency. Andrew had done everything he could, and it was out of his hands. God was in control.

"Hey, did you hear about Andy?" one of the guys from work said one day as they rode the ferry across to the mainland.

"A few months ago I heard he got a really good job and was doing well," Andrew said.

The guy shook his head. "No, I mean the new news. He *was* doing really well and making good money. But then he got mixed up with the wrong girl and got back into drugs. Got busted. He's back in jail."

Andrew's grin fell off his face. He'd been so happy for Andy and his great start on a new life on the street. Now he was back where he started. *Why does this keep happening?* he wondered. It made him more determined than ever to commit himself to the kind of life outside prison that would eliminate the possibility of him ever coming back to this place. *God, be with Andy,* Andrew prayed.

When December arrived, Andrew came down with a cold. It started with a sore throat and a cough, but the cold somehow grew teeth, and Andrew found himself in bed with a fever of 102°F. His chest hurt, and he had a headache from coughing so much. He alternated between sweating and shivering under his covers, and he knew he didn't have a typical winter cold.

"You have pneumonia," the doctor said after examining him. "You're going to the hospital on the mainland."

Andrew barely knew what was happening when they transported him off the island and admitted him into the hospital. He lay in his hospital bed, his body a lump of burning flesh.

"We're going to get your fever down and get you on some antibiotics," the nurse promised, squeezing his hand. "You're going to feel so much better."

On December 19, 2003, while Andrew lay in a hospital bed recovering from pneumonia, a clemency board met to decide Andrew's fate. Andrew knew that there were five members on the clemency panel, and three out of five of the members had to vote in his favor for him to be granted clemency. His mother, Mr. Smyly, and his attorney would argue in his favor, but the prosecutor who gave Andrew the plea bargain would also be there to testify against him on behalf of Andrew's victims. In the end, it all came down to a vote.

Andrew wasn't concerned. He knew that applying for clemency was what God wanted him to do. He'd seen the signs, he'd prayed, and he'd been convicted. It was only a matter of time before he would be a free man. He lay back against a wall of pillows and closed his eyes. He might as well get some rest. Any moment now they would come to tell him the good news.

If only his dad could see him now.

Chapter 20

A ndrew awoke in his hospital bed feeling much better. His temperature was down, and while he was still coughing and weak from the fever, he didn't feel as if his lungs were full of jelly anymore.

Why haven't they come to tell me the news from the clemency board? Andrew wondered. The television mounted in the corner of his room chattered noisily while Andrew stared out the window. It was dark, and the board should have made their decision a long time ago. *Maybe it is just taking time to process all the paperwork,* Andrew thought. He knew from experience that nothing in prison was ever done in a hurry. The staff seemed to operate at a different pace whenever Andrew was waiting for something, and to Andrew, that pace was painfully slow. He coughed into his elbow and sank back into his covers. Before long, the doctor came in.

"Did anyone leave a message for me?" Andrew asked.

The doctor shook his head. "Not that I know of, but I do have some good news. You're well enough to leave the hospital now. We've gotten your fever down and given your immune system a boost with antibiotics. We'll let your body take it from here." The doctor wrote on his pad, and then clicked his pen before tucking it into his coat pocket. "You take care of yourself, young man."

"Thanks," Andrew said, feeling perplexed.

The next day Andrew was back at McNeil Island. As soon as he could, he went to the phone and dialed his mom's number. She answered.

"I was waiting for you to call," she said.

"Oh, I've been sick," Andrew explained. "So how did it go?"

His mom sighed. "Andrew, they denied your clemency request."

"Denied?" Andrew couldn't believe what he was hearing. He had prayed about it. He felt God had planted the idea in his mind and given him signs to move forward with his application. Had he misunderstood?

"I did everything I could, Andrew," his mom said. He could hear disappointment in her voice. "Mr. Smyly gave you a wonderful recommendation; we had a good group there in support of you. The prosecutor seemed angry that you even applied for clemency, but the board reminded him that it was your right. Someone even brought up your infraction."

"My infraction? You mean when I said 'five-o' when I was 17 years old? That was years ago, and I've had model behavior ever since," Andrew said in disbelief.

"I know," his mom said. "All the board members had the chance to weigh in and say what they thought, and one of them mentioned that you'd paid your Legal Financial Obligation."

"Oh, brother. I was just lucky that *you* paid it for me. And all five voted against me?" Andrew asked, trying to swallow the news.

"No," his mom answered. "If there's any good news, it's that two of the five board members believed that you should be granted clemency. Two of them thought you'd earned it."

Disappointment stung Andrew's mind. One vote. He lost his chance to be set free early by one measly vote. And yet there was something empowering about knowing that two people on the board believed in him— two people believed, after reviewing his history, that he could reenter society and be a productive citizen. The loss was devastating and confusing to Andrew, but he dwelled on the idea that two of the votes were in his favor.

What do you do, Andrew wondered, *when you believe God has put something on your heart, and it doesn't happen? What if it doesn't come through?*

Andrew hadn't told any of his fellow prisoners that he'd applied for clemency, so when he heard about the loss, he had to swallow his disappointment alone. It was probably better that no one knew. That way he wouldn't have to explain what happened again and again; yet it was hard to carry the disappointment by himself.

Oh, well, Andrew thought. *I did everything I could do. And besides, I have only a few years left in this place before I've served my time and can go anyway.*

He tried to comfort himself with that thought, but knowing that he still had to face several more years after expecting to be freed felt as if a chain were around his neck. The strange thing was that he was still convicted that God had impressed him to apply for clemency. *Why would God have me apply, only to be denied?* Andrew wondered. *Maybe, somehow, some way, I'll still be granted clemency.*

That thought kept Andrew's hope alive every day as he worked and studied. He even wrote in his journal that he still believed he would be set free early, even though all the doors had shut and it looked as if it were over. *God,* Andrew prayed, *if I could just be released one day earlier . . . one day . . . that would be one more day I could spend doing something useful with my life.*

There were a lot of religious people in jail, and everyone wanted out. Everyone prayed to be released. Andrew knew that his own prayer was echoed in cells throughout the prison—other voices begged, "Hey, God, work a miracle and let me out." Andrew didn't know what God's plan was for his life or for the lives of the other prisoners, but he kept praying.

A few months later, to Andrew's dismay, the work camp shut down, and he had to go back to the main prison. He went back to his old job and shared a cell with his new cellmate, Kevin.

Kevin was the bitterest person Andrew had ever met, and Andrew soon found out why. One night Kevin had gotten drunk at a bar, and he was made to leave. He had been so angry about being kicked out of the bar that he had come back later with a gun and fired several rounds into the establishment. Andrew wasn't sure whether anyone had been killed during the incident, but Kevin was convicted and sentenced to a hefty prison term.

Dissatisfied with his representation and determined to overturn his sentence, Kevin studied the law books he could find, and decided to represent himself in an appeal. The appeals court reviewed his case and decided he was correct. They took 10 years off of his sentence.

Though his reduced sentence meant he only had seven more years behind bars, Kevin was not satisfied with the 10-year reduction, so he appealed again, this time through the Washington State Supreme Court. When that court reviewed his case, they again found out his sentencing was incorrect—only this time, it was not in his favor. The court told him that not only was his original sentence incorrect; his most recent sentence reduction was also incorrect. They put 20 years back on his sentence.

One day Kevin was trying to give legal advice to one of their fellow prisoners. The prisoner looked at Kevin and said, "I'm not taking advice from you! You're the one who got 20 years added to your sentence!"

Andrew had never seen Kevin angrier.

As "cellies," Andrew and Kevin learned to coexist in the same cell. It was the same routine every morning. Andrew would switch on his little light and read his Bible, while Kevin would wake up, get out of bed, open a can of Coca-Cola, and drink the whole thing. Then he'd poke holes in the can and stuff in some marijuana. After going over by the door to see where the guards were, Kevin would smoke his stash. Some mornings he'd shoot heroin while Andrew studied.

He'd sit on the floor and look up at Andrew. "Hey. You want some?"

"No," Andrew would always say.

Andrew had discovered early on that any drug available on the street was also available in prison. Tattoos were also available for a price. Tattoo artists would smuggle in a needle or a guitar string or file down a pen or a piece of metal. They also found ways of making ink, and they'd take apart radios and cassette players and use the insides to make a motor that would run the ink gun.

When they couldn't get alcohol, some of the prisoners would boil hand sanitizer and drink what remained, an idea that was disgusting to Andrew. It was apparently disgusting to the prisoners who tried to drink it, too.

"Man, I mixed it with a whole gallon of Kool-Aid," one of the guys told Andrew, "and it still scorched my throat. That stuff is nasty."

And yet, he drinks it, Andrew thought, shuddering. *There is a multitude of ways to get something done when you're sitting there all day long with nothing to do but think about how you can do what you want to do.*

Overall, Andrew got along with most people in prison. As a Christian, he avoided the behaviors that would get him into trouble, and he also kept himself busy. When necessary, he had no problem saying no. The other guys noticed that Andrew was different.

"Every day we see you studying and reading and going to the gym and the chapel all day long. You can't hide. We see everything you do. You're not a homosexual, you don't use drugs, you don't gamble, you've been in prison for about eight years, and you don't have even one tattoo," one of Andrew's fellow prisoners said to him.

"Those kinds of things attract problems," Andrew said. "I'm not looking for problems."

They were also amazed when they found out how long he'd spent in solitary confinement as a teenager. Some of the older prisoners would say, "Hey, Michell, is it true you were in the hole for two years? Man, your mind must be really messed up, dude. How did you deal with that?"

Andrew was open with them about his story and his evolving relationship with God. He was always ready to listen or to try to provide some encouragement.

One of his friends, Matthew, who was not a Christian, confided in him one day. "Andrew, it feels as though there's an intelligent force in my life that is trying to destroy me."

Andrew knew exactly what Matthew was talking about, because he'd also experienced it. They talked openly, and sometimes other prisoners listened in.

"Andrew, all you do all day is sit in the day room from 7:00 in the morning till 11:00 at night. That's all you do is study, study, study. You don't get involved in the homo stuff, you don't do dope, you're not telling on anybody, you're just doing your own thing, just minding your own business. You don't bother anybody, you just study and go to the church meeting. What are you going to do when you get out?" another guy asked him.

"I don't know what I'm going to do when I get out. I don't know anything about that world. This is all I know. I don't know what I want to *do*, but I know how I want to *live*. I want to live my life in such a way that no one would ever have any idea that I'd ever been in prison. I want to live a life that shows gratitude to the God who saved me and gave me life."

One day Andrew's welding teacher, who had not seen him for a few years while he was at work camp, overheard him talking to some of the other inmates. His teacher approached and said, "Wow! You're speaking!" He looked around and addressed the other guys in the group, "How did you get him to talk? He was in my class for a year, and I never heard him speak a word."

Andrew laughed. "I guess I have something to say," he answered. The truth was, Andrew couldn't help it. He understood what the prophet Jeremiah meant in Jeremiah 20:9 when he said, "His word burns in my heart like a fire. It's like a fire in my bones! I am weary of holding it in!"

Months passed, and Andrew got a new cellmate, Todd. Todd had a habit of affectionately calling Andrew "The Kid."

People would ask, "Todd, who is your cellie?"

Todd would answer, "Oh, I got The Kid. I got Andy."

Though Andrew was younger than Todd, they got along well and were always playing jokes on each other. Todd was impressed with Andrew's ability to say no all the time. Andrew said no to marijuana, alcohol, heroin, and tattoos. He also, however, said no when guys would come around asking for food or money. Andrew would refuse.

"It probably seems selfish," Andrew told Todd one day. "But these guys get their paychecks and squander them on useless things such as drugs or cigarettes, and then when they are hungry, they go around begging at cell doors. If I give them what they want they will never pay me back as they've promised, and I'll just be enabling their bad habits. I refuse to enable them."

Todd would always laugh. "You're the King of No!"

"Yeah, maybe," Andrew teased, "but I can't say no to your cookies. You'd better keep an eye on your locker. Robbie taught me how to solve a combination lock without the combination a few years ago. One of these days after you've been down there painting your ceramics, you might come back to find only crumbs."

"You can *not* do that!" Todd would say. Todd was very disciplined with his cookies. He could eat one, and then put the rest back into his locker to save for another time. He was not only disciplined, but he was very protective, and Andrew liked to tease him about it. Each time, Todd would respond the same way: "You can *not* take my cookies!"

January arrived with a burst of cold weather. It had been more than a year since his request for clemency was denied; however, with time off for good behavior and if nothing went wrong, Andrew would be released in September. In eight months his life would continue outside prison walls.

I just can't get into any trouble, Andrew thought. He'd seen it before. Guys who were scheduled for release somehow found themselves mixed up in trouble even though they didn't cause it and weren't even part of it. It would be an easy thing to get into trouble for something he didn't do. He'd have to be careful.

On January 11 Andrew was sitting in his cell when a guard appeared and called his name. "Andrew! Go down to the administration department. They want to see you *now.*"

Andrew swallowed. The last time he had been called down to the administration department, it was to find out his father had died. Todd looked up, and Andrew saw concern in his face, too.

Oh, man. What did I do wrong? he wondered. *Please, I can't get in trouble now. I only have eight more months to serve before I get out of here!*

As he walked out of his cell and turned the corner, an even worse thought occurred to him. *What if . . . something has happened to my mom?*

Trying to tame the panic that clawed the inside of his chest, Andrew made his way down to the administration office, wondering what news awaited him. Either he was going into the hole for something he was sure he didn't do or someone had died.

Chapter 21

Andrew walked down to administration in the bottom part of the cell-block in his unit. Before he even walked through the doorway, he could hear yelling. It was an argument between the lieutenant and a counselor no one liked.

Andrew stood in the doorway while the argument continued and watched the strange flurry of activity. It was odd. It actually looked as though the prison staff members were in a *hurry*. For the first time in years Andrew saw the prison officials up out of their chairs running around trying to get something done.

"Andrew—this guy—cannot be released until he has a preapproved release address!" the counselor yelled.

The lieutenant shook his head and his finger at the same time. "This guy just got a commutation from the governor. We got an order to release him. He doesn't need *anything*."

Whoa, what is all this about? Andrew wondered.

That's when the lieutenant apparently realized that Andrew was there. He ran over to Andrew, stuck his finger in his face, and said, "Are you Andrew Michell?"

Andrew nodded. "Yes?"

"We don't know who you are, and we don't know who you know, but we just got orders from Governor Gary Locke's office to release you immediately."

The lieutenant stepped back and stared at Andrew as though he were from the moon. "I have been working in this prison for years, and this has never happened to *anyone*. You need to go upstairs and pack up, because you're on the first boat out of here tomorrow morning."

I'm free? I'm going home tomorrow? Andrew couldn't quite comprehend the magnitude of what the lieutenant had just told him.

"Go pack," the lieutenant repeated.

Andrew turned and walked out of the administration office and back

125

up to his cell, E–405. By the time he got upstairs, he was so giddy he could hardly contain himself.

Todd was happy for him. "Tomorrow is Governor Locke's last day in office," Todd said. "Signing your commutation must have been one of the last official things he did as governor. But how did he know about you?"

"I have no idea," Andrew said. "I can't figure it out. Maybe someone from that clemency hearing a year ago told him about me. I don't know— but I'm not complaining!"

Andrew found out about his commutation at 3:00 p.m. He immediately packed his stuff in a box, knowing that only one night stood between him and his freedom. It would be the longest night of his life.

"So what are you going to do first?" one of the other prisoners said when he found out about Andrew's release. "Get laid? Get drunk?"

"I'm not doing any of that," Andrew said. "I'm a Christian. God is giving me this opportunity, and I intend to use it to do all the good I can do."

Some of the guys gave him a hard time, but Andrew didn't care. That night, before he went to bed, Andrew wrote a letter to his Savior:

"Lord Jesus,
"Thank You so much! I received news that my release date has been moved to tomorrow! *Thank You.* I have been asking You for an early release for years, and You came through. Thank You so much! As You know, many challenges await me: money, career, play, education, family, sex, drugs, church, friends, my past . . . Please help me every step of the way. Don't allow me to drift or lose the focus I have placed on knowing You. I am trusting You to use me to do so much good. Thanks.
"I love You, Jesus.
"Andrew Michell"

Andrew didn't sleep that night. He was too excited. He lay on the top bunk staring at the ceiling, waiting for the hours to pass while Todd slept in the bunk below him. *H'mmm,* Andrew thought. *I've got to play some kind of prank on Todd. It's my last one, so I've got to make it good. What can I do?*

Todd got up and went to work at 7:00 a.m., and Andrew remained in the cell. The night before, he'd come up with the perfect prank. As soon as Todd left, Andrew got up and went over to Todd's locker. Using the technique Robbie had showed him, Andrew managed to solve the combination lock and Todd's locker came open. There, on the shelf, were Todd's prized cookies. Andrew sat down on the bed and munched on cookies until he'd eaten the last one. Then he sprinkled cookie crumbs on

Todd's desk and his bed. Then he took all of Todd's socks and tied them together, along with his bedding, his floss, and his shoelaces. Then he scribbled a note on a piece of paper and put it where Todd would find it when he got back from work: "You can *not* tell me what to do anymore!"

Andrew knew that if he told his mom or anyone else on the outside, they would think it was a mean prank. But nobody else knew Todd's sense of humor or the kind of friendship they shared. Andrew knew Todd would probably want to wring his neck, but he'd still get a kick out of it.

After completing his prank, Andrew sat down and waited. Normally, when prisoners were released, it happened around 7:00 or 8:00 in the morning, and they took the first boat off the island. The hours passed while Andrew waited in his cell, and still no one came to get him. *They probably just don't know how to handle this kind of unusual release,* he thought.

As far as he could remember during his time in prison, he had never known anyone who received a commutation. Many times prisoners were released early for good behavior. The law had the authority to grant prisoners "good time," as long as they didn't beat anyone up or kill anyone or do any of the other thousands of things that were prohibited. Because of the seriousness of Andrew's crime, the percentage of time off he could have received was very small, but some prisoners were able to leave several months or even years early. But before they could be released, they had to have an address that a parole officer could inspect to make sure it was a safe place to be.

In other words, Andrew thought, *not a marijuana farm or a methamphetamine lab.*

If the prisoner was a pedophile, his address couldn't be close to an elementary school. Many of the prisoners arrived at their early release date, but because they'd lost all of their friends and their family wanted nothing to do with them, they had no preapproved release address to go to, and they had to stay in prison until they could obtain one.

That's what the lieutenant and the counselor had been arguing about the day before when Andrew had arrived at the office. The lieutenant was correct, however; because Andrew had a commutation directly from the governor, they had to release him without a preapproved address.

So what's taking so long? Andrew thought, resisting the urge to chew his fingernails.

"Oh, it's you," he heard a voice say. He looked up to see one of the counselors standing by his cell looking in. "I heard that someone got a commutation, and I had to come by and see who it was. I didn't know your name, because you've never been in trouble. You didn't stand out," she laughed. "Congratulations."

More than once as the day wore on, prison officials came by his cell just to look at him—probably because they were amazed at what had happened.

Andrew waited hour after hour for his paperwork to be processed. He knew that things moved slowly in the Department of Corrections. It could take weeks to get anything approved. From the state employees' perspective there was no reason to move any faster, and there was nothing the prisoners could do about it because they were locked up.

Finally, later that afternoon, a guard arrived to escort him out. Andrew took a deep breath and stood up, holding his box of possessions. They walked down the cellblock, through the maze of hallways and doors, until they were outside. Andrew's heart pounded with excitement as he followed the guard down to the main gate of the prison. He'd walked down here before when he worked at the camp, but this time was different. The gate actually opened up for them; Andrew and the guard walked out, and it shut behind him.

I never have to go back, Andrew thought, glancing over his shoulder at the austere concrete buildings behind him that got smaller with every step.

Andrew and the guard walked down the hill to the waiting boat. The guard sat next to him as the boat drudged slowly through the waters of the sound, ferrying them to the other side. They stepped off the boat, then walked up the ramp and to the little boathouse.

Andrew looked ahead and saw a yellow line painted on the cement. He stared at it as it got closer. *When I walk across that line, I'm free.*

Andrew stepped over the yellow line, and for the first time in more than 10 years the guard turned around without a word and walked away. Andrew stood there, unguarded and unchained. No further relationship with the Department of Corrections. Not even parole. It was January 12, 2005, nine months earlier than his official release date, and Andrew was a free man.

When he looked up, he saw his mom. She held out her arms as he walked toward her, and Andrew gave her a big hug. Neither one of them could say much of anything. They got into the truck and started driving down Steilacoom Boulevard, then to South Tacoma Way, and then to the onramp for Highway 512 toward the city of Puyallup.

Andrew gripped the handle on the door. As his mom accelerated the truck to merge onto the highway, Andrew suddenly had the sensation that he was in a roller coaster, gradually climbing the incline and cresting the pinnacle, just about to go over . . .

Hundreds of cars and SUVs and semis whizzed past them on the highway, and Andrew felt dizzy as the trees and straw-colored grass blurred by. His stomach felt as if it were floating dangerously close to his throat, and he felt panic closing in.

"Mom!" he yelled, "Why are you going so *fast?* Slow *down!*"

Andrew's mom smiled at him with a strange look on her face. "Andrew, the speed limit is 60, and I'm doing 60. I'm not speeding."

Andrew felt paranoid as the world rushed by him on all sides. *So many people. So many cars. Everyone is going so fast. Why are there so many people driving so fast?* He tried to calm down and breathe. *You haven't been on a highway in a decade,* he reminded himself. Still, he gripped the door with white-knuckled fingers, and didn't let go until his mom had pulled into the mall parking lot and eased into a parking space.

"You're going to need some clothes," his mom said. "Let's go shop for some jeans and a new shirt."

The area around South Hill Mall had changed. New restaurants and stores had appeared, and some of the familiar places were gone. As they walked through the side door of JCPenney, Andrew grimly remembered the last time he had been there. He and his friend had challenged themselves to steal something from every store without getting caught. They had been successful. Andrew felt slightly sick.

"You go check out the jeans, and I'll look at shirts," his mom said.

Andrew felt lost as he stood alone in the men's department. For the past 10 years all he'd had was one pair of pants—just a pair of jeans that he wore every day. He never had to think about what to wear. He turned to the right and walked toward the signs until he stood in front of a giant wall with rows and rows of blue jeans. The cubbyholes each had numbers written on them: 32 x 34. 34 x 36. 34 x 30. Baggy jeans. Bootcut jeans. Relaxed fit jeans. Pleated jeans. Jeans with no pleats. Dark blue. Light blue. Khaki. It was overwhelming. He had no idea what size he wore, and he felt paralyzed by the choices.

"Paralysis by analysis," he whispered to himself as he stared at the wall of what seemed like a million choices. He didn't know what to do, so he just stood there.

He smelled her before he saw her. It had been years since he smelled a woman's perfume. A female sales associate walked up to him and smiled. It was also the first time in 10 years that a woman had walked into his 36 inches of personal space.

"Can I help you?" she said, looking into his face.

Andrew couldn't look back. She was standing too close to him. The jeans, the saleswoman—it was all too much. He reached up and grabbed the first random pair of jeans he touched. "This is what I want," he mumbled, and hurried away from the saleswoman, who stared after him as he pushed through the racks of clothes to leave.

Andrew found his mom by the cash register. "Mom, here. Let's just get these and get out of here."

His mom smiled as she took the jeans from him. "OK, we'll get these. But let's walk around the mall a little bit first. Are you hungry? I'm hungry. Let's get something to eat."

Andrew was in no mood to eat, but he agreed to go to the food court. Walking beside his mom, he made it through the first arm of the mall, past the vitamin supplement store, left at the information booth, and down the length of the north end of the mall to the food court.

When they arrived at the food court, it was sensory overload for Andrew. So many people filled the mall—walking by, brushing past him, talking and laughing loudly. Clothing styles were new and strange and shocking, and body parts were showing that he hadn't seen in 10 years. Everyone seemed to be talking on a cell phone. The constant offers from salespeople at kiosks and the discordant electronic melodies blasting out of the video arcade and the smells from each individual food eatery came crashing into his senses. It was too much. He broke down.

"Mom, we gotta go."

"Why?" his mom asked. "Don't you want to get something to eat?"

Andrew panicked. "Mom, let's *go*. Now. I've got to go *now*."

Andrew knew his behavior was probably strange and unnerving to his mom. She didn't say much when they got back into the truck and began to drive. Every so often she'd glance at him with a worried look on her face, and he felt bad for making her uncomfortable by his actions. But he knew there was no way he could possibly help her understand what it was like to be bombarded with so much stimuli after so many years locked in a concrete jungle. This strange new world was going to require a whole different set of survival skills than what he'd used to navigate prison life.

On the way home, Andrew felt another unexpected sensation—a huge sense of dread. He didn't want to go back to that house. There were too many bad memories. He felt afraid of stepping into the same environment he'd walked out of the night he'd been arrested 10 years ago. That's where the arguments with his parents had occurred. That's where his brothers had died. That's where he'd lived when he had been actively engaged in crime, and stashed throughout that house were stolen reminders of his former life.

In prison, at least, he had been learning and advancing and maturing. Now as they turned onto familiar streets that led him toward home, he hated the idea of going back there. It made his skin crawl. *Can I still be the*

kind of Christian I was in prison when I'm bombarded with all my old surround-
ings and memories and feelings?

They pulled into the driveway, and Andrew's mom took the keys out of the ignition. "Well," she said, smiling, "here we are. I'll have to show you the new garage your dad built behind the house. Not much else has changed."

Andrew slowly stepped out of the truck and looked up at the house.

"Come on, Andrew," his mom said. "Stand over there by the bushes and let me get your picture holding your 'Get Out of Jail Free Card.'"

Andrew picked his commutation papers from the governor up off the seat of the truck and smiled as he posed next to the bushes for a picture. Then he picked up his small box of possessions and followed his mom up the steps. She unlocked the door and swung it open, and Andrew stepped inside.

Andrew paused and looked around. The furniture was new and things had been moved around, but the smell of home still held a vague familiarity. He wandered through the house, looking into the rooms, until he got to his own bedroom and pushed the door open. He set his box down on the floor and took it all in. His mom had placed everything in plastic containers that lined his room in stacks. His bed was still in the corner.

"Andrew!" his mom called. "You must be starving. What do you want to eat? I'll cook you anything you want."

Andrew quietly walked down the hall to the kitchen. The floor still creaked in all the familiar places. But the walls had been painted a different color.

His mom opened the refrigerator wide and motioned for him to look. "What do you want to eat?" she asked.

Andrew looked down into the refrigerator; it was packed with food. There was food stacked everywhere in all the compartments—all kinds of food. So many options. Too many options.

Once again, Andrew felt overwhelmed. For a decade he had eaten whatever vegetarian version of industrial-grade food was slapped on his tray at mealtime, except for the jar of peanut butter he bought with the money he'd earned, and the cans of tuna he had kept in his locker. Now he stared at fresh vegetables, fruits, condiments, Tupperware containers, deli meats, and a host of other items.

Just then Andrew saw a can of tuna on one of the racks. "I'll eat that," he said.

"OK, just let me cut up some pickles. I'll mix it with some mayonnaise, and I've got some bread here . . ." His mom reached into the refrigerator for the tuna and the pickle jar.

"No, thanks," Andrew said, "I'll just eat it plain. Out of the can."

"What?" his mom said, looking at him as if trying to decide if he was serious. "Out of the can? With nothing else?"

Andrew nodded. "Yeah."

His mom stood there with her hand on her hip for a moment, and then nodded. "OK, then. Well, at least let me put it in a bowl for you."

She carefully scooped the tuna out of the can, put it in a bowl, and handed it to Andrew along with a spoon. Ironically, with all of the options he had available to him from a refrigerator packed with food, Andrew's first meal when he got out of prison was a can of tuna.

That night he took off his clothes and crawled into his old bed in his own room. It felt so strange. After sleeping on a hard, thin little mattress in prison, the mattress on his bed at home was just too fluffy and soft, and he couldn't get comfortable.

God, Andrew prayed. *What is happening to me? For 10 years all I wanted was to get out of prison. I begged You for it. I dreamed about it. It was everything I wanted. And now that I'm finally free, I feel so out of place. Don't get me wrong. I'm grateful for everything You've done. But tonight . . . I kind of wish I was back in my cell, where everything is familiar. I knew who I was there. Now I've got to try to figure out who the free version of Andrew is, and I'm so overwhelmed by everything; I don't know if I can.*

Andrew tossed and turned for a while, and then sat up and stared at the wall. His back hurt from the fluffy mattress, and part of him felt like an insecure little kid. He remembered what Michael Jackson, his first cellie in adult prison, had told him—that he'd felt like a martian when he was released from prison the first time. Andrew had thought the guy was crazy then, but now he understood. Freedom after such a long stint in captivity tasted bittersweet.

He stood up and pulled his blanket and pillow off the bed. He arranged them on the carpet and then lay down on the floor with only a thin covering. He lay there for a long time. And then, finally, he closed his eyes and fell asleep.

Chapter 22

Early the next morning Andrew's mom poked her head in through his open doorway and looked down at Andrew on the floor.

"You slept on the floor?" she asked, looking around at the bedding and pillows on the carpet. "Is something wrong with your bed?"

"No," Andrew said. "I just felt like sleeping on the floor."

His mom seemed bewildered, but she didn't press him about it. "Well, I'm headed to work. Are you going to be OK here by yourself?"

"Yeah, I'm fine," Andrew said. "I'll see you later."

"I could call in and stay home today if you need me to."

"No," Andrew said. "I'll be fine."

Hesitantly his mom said goodbye, and a moment later Andrew heard the truck start. The engine noise grew fainter, and then the house was silent. Andrew looked around the room. *What now?* he thought.

Andrew got up, padded down the hallway, and went to the kitchen. After opening up several cupboard doors, he finally managed to find a bowl and some cereal. As he ate, he looked out the back window at the five-car garage his father had built before he died.

Slowly he made his way around the house. Everywhere he looked he saw stacked plastic boxes. His mom had preserved everything. His things, his father's things, family mementos, newspaper clippings, correspondence, every item relating to Andrew's incarceration—it was all there.

She must have been afraid to throw this stuff away, Andrew thought. *I've got to help her go through it and get rid of it.*

Even though the plastic boxes were organized and stacked, they were taking up physical space in the house—and Andrew feared they were taking up emotional space for his mom as well. Andrew was anxious not only to help his mom clear away unnecessary items but also anxious to comb through the house and eliminate stolen items he'd collected during his years of crime. When he'd read the story of Achan, he made a promise to God and had waited for the chance to be able to clear the house of the cursed things. He felt that when the house was purged, *then* he'd be truly free.

Let's see, Andrew thought. *I need to work on downsizing the plastic boxes Mom saved. I need to get my driver's license. I have to go down to Pierce College and see what classes I still need to take to earn my degree. I also want to find a church to attend . . .*

Andrew saw a phone book on the counter. He sat down and flipped through the pages. *Let's see, Assisted Living, Auto Parts, Bail Bonds—don't need that,* Andrew thought. *Car Repair, Carpentry, Child Care . . . ah, here we are. Churches.*

Andrew ran his thumb down the list of denominations. When he got to the letter *S,* he sat back in surprise. *Seventh-day Adventist? There's a Seventh-day Adventist church in Puyallup? Right here where I live? I thought I was going to have to travel a long way to find one!* Andrew was elated.

Wow, he thought as he looked at the listings. *There are a lot of them. I guess I was mistaken when I thought only a few Adventists existed. I should call and see if I can get a hold of the people from Yelm who held church for us at the prison.*

Andrew's finger shook as he dialed the number for the Puyallup church and waited for the call to go through. A moment later a woman's voice answered. It was the secretary.

"Hi," Andrew said hesitantly. "I'm looking for information. I'm try-ing to contact the Yelm Seventh-day Adventist Church."

"Well, you've called at the right time," the church secretary said. "There's someone from the Yelm church here right now. Her name is Sheila."

"Sheila!" Andrew said, "I know Sheila. Tell her it's Andrew Michell!"

A moment later Andrew heard Sheila's excited voice on the other end of the line. They talked for several minutes, and before they hung up, Sheila arranged for Pastor Kieth to come to his house to visit him.

The next day Pastor Kieth knocked on the door, and Andrew invited him in. Andrew explained to him that he'd just gotten out of prison, but that he'd been studying the Bible and he wanted to join the Seventh-day Adventist Church.

Pastor Kieth seemed happy to hear that, and he began to ask Andrew questions. "What do you know about Bible doctrine?" he asked. "Do you know about the Sabbath?"

"Yeah!" Andrew said, "I studied with Doug Batchelor for two years. Well, kind of. I listened to *Bible Answers Live* while I was in prison, and then I met with a Seventh-day Adventist study group later at McNeil Island."

After some other questions, Pastor Kieth said, "What do you know about the Spirit of Prophecy?"

"The spirit of what?" Andrew asked. "What is that?"

"Have you ever read anything by Ellen White?" Pastor Kieth asked.

"Yeah!"

"What did you read?"

"The first book I read was called *Counsels on Diet and Foods.*"

Pastor Kieth looked surprised. "Well, who gave you that?"

"A guy from the Bible study group. That was the best book I've ever read!"

Andrew enjoyed his visit with Pastor Kieth, but he decided he didn't want to go to church his first week out of prison. He was still getting used to his surroundings, and felt it would be best to wait a week. Pastor Kieth understood and said he looked forward to seeing him there the following week.

When Sabbath morning of the following week arrived, Andrew got ready for church and drove to the address that Pastor Kieth had given him. He was excited and nervous as he parked the car, got out, and walked to the front door. As he stepped into the foyer, he wanted to kneel down and kiss the carpet, which he knew would be a little silly and would probably freak out the older woman who came over to greet him, but he was excited about his first real Sabbath in a real Seventh-day Adventist church.

"How are you?" the sweet-faced grandmotherly type asked as she shook his hand and gave him a church bulletin. "Are you looking for Sabbath school?"

"Yeah, I think so," Andrew said, uncertain.

"Well, you look young. Would you like to meet with the high school students or the young adults?" the woman smiled at him.

"Uh, I don't know," Andrew stammered. *This is so weird,* he thought. *In prison everyone knew I was a prisoner. Everyone knew I was a felon and a creep and a loser and the scum of society. I wonder if this nice little old woman can tell. Is it written on my forehead?*

Andrew wasn't sure if he should confess to being an ex-con or not. Should he tell her? Did she already know? Andrew felt paralyzed by the dilemma. Finally he blurted out, "Uh, uh, I don't know what to do. Listen, I just got out of prison. I've been in prison for the past 10 years. I really don't know where to go. Can you please just show me where to go?"

At that moment a young man in a suit walked up to greet them, and the woman motioned in his direction. "Well, this is our youth pastor, Pastor William. Maybe you should talk to him."

Pastor William introduced himself, and then said, "What's your name? Where are you from?"

Immediately Andrew blurted out again, "I just got out of prison. I've been in prison for the past 10 years. I really don't know what to do. I'm kind of lost. Can you just show me where to go? Can I just sit down somewhere?"

"Sure," Pastor William said. "Follow me."

Andrew followed him to a room marked "Young Adults" and stood there nervously as Pastor William introduced him to a nice guy named Tom. Unsure of what to do, Andrew blurted out the same thing to Tom that he'd told Pastor William and the greeter.

Tom smiled at him as though he hadn't heard any of Andrew's confession about just getting out of prison. "Great," Tom said. "Come on in and sit down."

I've got to slow down on telling everyone I just got out of prison, Andrew told himself. After that, except for Jeremy and Christina, a young couple he became good friends with, Andrew didn't tell anyone else.

During his first few weeks at home, Andrew gradually began to adjust to life outside of prison. He had lost contact with his old friends, including Lina. Andrew heard that she'd gotten married and moved away. She was probably a mom by now. *A lot happened while I was gone,* Andrew thought. Life outside of prison hadn't waited around for him, that's for sure.

One of the first things Andrew put on his to-do list was to write a "thank you" e-mail to now ex-Governor Gary Locke. "I don't know why you did this," Andrew wrote, "but I just want you to know that I'm thankful beyond any means that I can express." He hoped he'd receive a response that explained how his commutation came to be, but Andrew never heard back from the former governor.

Andrew also began to systematically go through each of the plastic containers, tossing items they didn't need anymore and saving only the really important things. Andrew made several trips to the dump—so many, in fact, that he got to know the girl at the dump on a first-name basis.

"Andrew, we should really go to lunch or something—hang out sometime," she said one afternoon when he stopped at the weigh station to pay. Her chin was cupped in her palm, and she was smiling at him.

Andrew suddenly felt very shy. "Yeah, yeah," he said. "That would be great."

Was she flirting with me? he wondered as he drove away. No girl had flirted with him in more than a decade, and he wasn't sure he'd recognize it if it happened—or even what to do about it. *I can't possibly go to lunch with her. The guys were right,* Andrew thought miserably. *I haven't dealt with this since I was a teenager. Normal life stopped when I went to prison, and now I feel like a 16-year-old kid in a 26-year-old man's body! Will I ever figure this out?*

Andrew went home and picked up another plastic container to sort through. As he leafed through papers and photos and old VHS tapes, Andrew suddenly stopped. There was a VHS tape in the bottom of the container that he recognized. He picked it up and stared at it for a moment before he unfolded his legs from their crisscross sitting position and walked across the room. He put the videotape into the VCR and pushed the "Play" button.

A strange feeling crept over him as he watched. He remembered videotaping the footage on the tape right after his mom had purchased the video camera. He must have been 15 or 16, a matter of weeks before his arrest. No one else had been home at the time, and Andrew had taken the video camera on a tour of the house. Now, an audience of his own video, Andrew watched the guided tour of each room. *I remember doing this,* he thought.

Just then on the screen, the video camera momentarily captured young Andrew's face in the mirror as he was taping. Andrew gasped as he looked at the teenage version of himself. His face had a demonic hard edge, his lips were pulled back into a sneer and his eyes . . . something awful about his eyes . . . Andrew immediately jumped up and ejected the tape from the machine. His hands shook as he held the videotape. He'd come face to face with himself. He'd literally seen his old reflection as in a mirror, and it was so disturbing, Andrew couldn't stand to look at it.

That's not me anymore, Andrew said to himself. *I'm not that person anymore. I have Jesus in me now.*

Impulsively, he lifted the plastic guard and began ripping the ribbon out of the tape. When he got to the end of the ribbon, he decided it wasn't enough. He scooped up the pile of twisted ribbon off the floor, along with the plastic videocassette, and took it outside to the fire pit. He set it on fire and burned it until all that was left was a pile of ashes. The old Andrew was gone.

Andrew went back inside the house. That videotape brought back so many memories. He remembered the arguments he had had with his dad. He remembered cutting himself with the scissors right there in the kitchen while his parents watched. He remembered shrugging his dad's hand off his shoulder in the living room the morning they found Chris. He remembered demanding a car and physically threatening his parents. Andrew felt terrible. Sure, God had forgiven him of all that while he was still in prison. But here in this house, the memories lingered.

Andrew knelt down on the floor next to the plastic container and continued to sort through papers. At the bottom, he found a note in his father's handwriting.

What's this? Andrew wondered. He unfolded it.

In the upper right hand corner, it said, "The Lake, October 2001." It was a letter from his dad to his mom. Andrew began to read:

Dear Kathy,

For the first time in many years, I'm at peace knowing that Andrew will make something of his life, and I will not have to be ashamed for my actions or his.

It is quiet here, and I wish you and I could be fishing together.

Love,

Don XO

Andrew read it again and again, kneeling on the floor in the living room. Those few short sentences answered questions that had agonized Andrew's mind since the moment he learned of his father's death. Now he knew, and a huge weight fell off of him. His father had forgiven him, and he knew that someday Andrew would do things that would make him proud, even if he wasn't around to see it.

"Rest in peace, Dad," Andrew whispered as he held the letter. "I love you."

Chapter 23

The counselor at Pierce College looked at the computer screen and then back at Andrew. "You have more than 200 college credits, and you have a 3.67 GPA," he said, his voice flat with incredulity.

"Yes, I know," Andrew said, sitting across the desk in the counseling office with his papers. It was a few days before spring quarter began, and Andrew was at the college to register for classes.

The counselor sat back in his chair. "I have never had a student sit in my office with this many credits on his transcript before," he continued. He looked back at the screen and ran his index finger over the mouse. "You only need 90 credits to graduate with a degree," he said. "However, let me see, it looks as though many of your credits were toward vocational training, so there are still some classes you need to take to fulfill a Direct Transfer Degree, which is what you want, I assume?"

"Yes," Andrew said. "I'd really like to transfer to the University of Washington."

The counselor nodded. "Let's get you going on those missing classes for your degree, and you'll graduate next spring. If all goes well, you could be at UW next fall."

On the first day of classes Andrew looked down at his schedule and shifted his backpack over his shoulder. *Precalculus I, English Composition, and Survey of Physics.* It was so strange to be on an actual college campus with swarms of students buzzing past him on all sides as he made his way to his precalculus class. He walked through the doorway and chose a seat near the front of the class. All of the other students were sitting around talking and laughing with each other. Even though they weren't paying attention specifically to him, Andrew couldn't shake the feeling that he had "ex-con" written on his forehead, and that everyone knew his history.

You're just a regular student, Andrew reminded himself. *Act like one.*

The professor came into class, and the noise quieted as he began to read the list of names on the roster. When he came to Andrew's name, he paused. "Mr. Michell?" he asked, pronouncing it "MITCH-ull."

Andrew raised his hand, and the teacher looked up at him. "Is that how you pronounce your name?" the professor asked.

"Uh, no," Andrew said. "It's actually Michell, like the girl's name, Michelle. Andrew Michell."

The teacher made a note and continued down the roster, but Andrew had a weird feeling about the exchange regarding his name. He couldn't place the source of the feeling exactly, but it seemed important, as though something was going to happen because of those few moments in class spent emphasizing his name.

At the end of class Andrew gathered up his papers and his book and walked out of the classroom. Before he'd taken two steps down the hallway, a student from his precalculus class came up to him.

"Hey," he said, falling into stride with Andrew. "Is your name Andrew Michell?"

"Yes."

"Did you have a brother named Christopher?"

Andrew looked over at him. "Yes," he said again.

The guy nodded. "I thought so. I remember you."

Andrew stopped walking and turned to face him. "You do?" he asked.

"Yeah," the guy continued. "The last time I saw you, it was Halloween night. Man, it must have been around 1993 or 1994. You were out trick-or-treating in the neighborhood near my house. You went up to this one house to trick-or-treat, and you were upset because the man didn't give you enough candy. You were so mad that you broke the window in his car and took his radio."

Andrew sighed. Unfortunately, he remembered that event well. It must have been the Halloween before he was arrested, while Chris was still alive.

"By the way," the guy said, sticking out his hand. "I'm Sean."

"Hey, what are you doing later, after classes?" Andrew asked, grinning at Sean and shaking his hand. "I want to tell you a story."

So there was a reason for the exchange about my name, he thought when Sean agreed to meet up with him after classes. *God must want Sean to hear the story of how He changed me from the kid Sean remembers into the person I am now.*

Later that day Andrew told Sean the whole story of how he was arrested, how he went to prison, and how he found God. Sean listened intently and seemed amazed as Andrew shared the story with him. Andrew knew that God had given him this chance, and it was all because his professor had mispronounced his name.

Andrew knew there had been a reason to share his story with Sean, but he also knew it was probably best to keep his past to himself with everyone else. The fact that he'd been in prison was embarrassing, and he didn't want other people to know about the stupid things he'd done as a kid. Now that he was free, he wanted to live as a fully free person, without the stigma of prison following him around.

It was when he tried to have conversations with other students, however, that Andrew became painfully aware of the social nuances he'd lost while in prison. Some of the students would talk and joke about things he didn't understand; and some of the things that were funny to say in prison weren't funny in a group of college students. Andrew endured more than one awkward silence because his sense of humor fell flat in his new circle of acquaintances. To complicate matters, when girls approached him in a flirtatious way, Andrew felt like a shy, tongue-tied teenager.

Will I ever figure this out? Andrew wondered.

One day Andrew sat at one of the computers in the library at school, working on a paper for his English Composition class, when a girl came and sat down at the computer next to him. He didn't make eye contact with her—a habit leftover from prison—but he could see out of the corner of his eye that she was young and pretty, and she smelled like a bowl of fresh fruit.

He could feel her looking at him, but he kept staring at his computer screen, trying to concentrate on his research. After a few minutes she scooted her chair closer to him and leaned in his direction.

What is she doing? Andrew asked himself. He clicked on a link and continued reading the words on the screen. He realized she was looking at him, and then at his computer screen, and then back at him. *Is she trying to get my attention?* he wondered. *What do I do? Should I say something?*

Finally the girl reached into her purse and held a stick of gum toward him. "Would you like a piece of gum?" she asked, leaning closer to him. By now she was practically touching him.

"Uh, yes," Andrew said, quickly taking the gum and popping it into his mouth. He chewed furiously. "Thank you," he added, still not looking at her.

A minute or so later the girl sighed heavily, grabbed her purse, and stormed out of the library. Andrew continued chewing furiously. *I think I handled that wrong,* he told himself. *This is going to take some work.*

The weeks of spring quarter passed quickly, and one of Andrew's final assignments in his English class was an interview paper. He was to find someone to write about, conduct an interview, and then write a paper about the person he interviewed. Andrew knew right away whom he would contact—his friend Brian from prison.

For a change, Andrew was on the *receiving* end of a prison phone call, and Brian was more than happy to answer Andrew's interview questions. When the call ended—abruptly with a click, of course, exactly 20 minutes later—Andrew sat down and wrote his paper. He decided to title it "#971988," which was Brian's inmate identification number in prison.

The next day when Andrew handed his paper to his professor, Mr. Mohrbacher glanced at the title and looked up at Andrew with a puzzled expression. "What is this?"

"Oh," Andrew said, "I got in contact with this guy in prison and interviewed him and wrote about him."

Instead of tossing the paper on the pile with the others, Mr. Mohrbacher looked down at the page and started to read. Andrew waited nervously as his teacher read:

#971988

"A whole $52.50, that is how much I make a month. No, I know it is nothing to really brag about, but I manage to get by. Usually I spend it all on junk food, though I sometimes save up a few dollars here and there to buy a pair of sneakers or a cassette tape. I really cannot complain; all I have to do for 40 cents an hour is push the dirty laundry cart over to the laundry room and bring it back when everything is clean. Now that I have topped out on the pay scale for the past several years, I can always tell you exactly how much I get paid. But it really is not about the money; I just like having something to do to keep me busy. I have been in prison now for almost 14 years, and keeping busy helps me do something productive with my time and focus on a better future.

"My crime was so stupid and senseless. My cousin and I had been out all night drinking and barhopping in the Cedar Ponds area of Monroe. Once the bars began to close, we headed out to an after-hours party in the woods. After more drinking, my cousin got into a fight with another guy at the party. The other guy pulled out a knife, and I tried to get the knife away. I jumped on the guy, wrestled for the knife, and ended up stabbing him twice. He was airlifted to Harborview with a punctured lung and severed liver. Because he survived, I was arrested for attempted murder. It was September 1992, and within a few months I was tried, convicted, and sentenced to almost 19 years in prison. I was only 22 years old.

"Until that night, I had never got in any serious trouble. Sure, I did not meet the criteria for an outstanding citizen award, but I definitely was not a criminal that lurked about waiting to commit acts of violence. Before the incident, I never exhibited any violent behavior. I was just a 22-year-old working alcoholic. I made it as far as the ninth grade before I quit school to do concrete and iron construction work. I worked, drank, and functioned at an acceptable level, but I never went around looking to hurt people.

"Fourteen years: that is how long I have been without any family, friends, or freedom. I have spent my entire adult life in this human wasteland that in no way reflects the reality that everyone else in the world takes for granted. Every single day I wake up without fail to the same misery and insanity, to breathe the same stale air saturated with the foul funk of hopelessness. Imagine living in here for just 14 days, or even 14 hours.

"When I was arrested, Bill Clinton was still campaigning for the presidency and *Roseanne* was one of America's favorite prime time television shows. In the year I went to prison, riots broke out in Los Angeles over the beating of Rodney King, and the movie *Aladdin* received an Academy Award. I cannot comprehend why people commit crimes and come back to this place after being released. The average prison sentence is only about two years, yet I have seen the same people return to prison again and again. They spend their life in and out of the system, indifferent to any opportunities to straighten out their life. All I want is just one chance to get my life back.

"After all this, I just cannot look at life in the same way. My time is my only true possession, and once it is gone, it is gone forever. That is why I am so glad my release date is only a couple years away. I have been waiting for January 15, 2008, for a very long, long time, and now I am finally a 'short-timer.' In here I have learned to focus on how important life really is because it will tend to just go on without you. Just a few days ago a man in here came to the point where he could not handle it any longer, so he went in his cell and hung himself. He was only doing a few years. A while back another guy with a life sentence did a swan dive off the top tier and landed on his head on the concrete. The poor fool lived, and now he will spend the rest of his life in prison as a quadriplegic. We can all justify our reason for giving up, but I continue to hold on to the possibility of a better future. If my victim would have died, I would have been charged with manslaughter and sentenced to only eight years and out in six, but I decided long ago that I am not going to let this place be the end of me. No matter how bleak things may seem, it is never really THAT bad.

"Nowadays all I can think about is Alaska. I have watched every television show and read every map, pamphlet, and available book in the library system on the Last Frontier. When this kid from college was interviewing me, he thought he would impress me by telling me he just read Jon Krakauer's *Into the Wild* in his English class. Yeah, I read that. In fact, there is not much I do not know about Alaska. No, I have never been there, but I would sure like to settle down there someday. Alaska seems to be somewhere to get away from all the people and the hectic lifestyle. All this madness around here: I do not really care for any of it. I want to get out, get my life together, and have a family of my own. I want a house with a roof that doesn't leak.

"In here I am #971988, another faceless dead man among the thousands of nobodies. Once I walk out that door, I will just be another average Joe swallowed up in a mass of 6 billion people, but out there, I will have a name. I will say hello to my neighbor, and he will call me Brian."

Mr. Mohrbacher looked up at Andrew. "Wow," he said. "You actually interviewed this guy over the phone?"

"Yeah," Andrew said.

"That must have been scary. Imagine if you were actually in the prison sitting with this guy. That would have really been scary."

Andrew tried to suppress a grin. He wondered what his professor would think if he knew that he had been in prison for years and that Brian was actually one of his good friends. It was bizarre to think about it from the professor's perspective, since Brian was someone Andrew had lived with in prison for so long and knew so well. "Yeah," he said, trying not to laugh. "That would be frightening."

Andrew finished spring quarter and signed up for new classes. Each day he felt a little more acclimated to the outside world, and while he missed his friends from prison, he began to feel more at home in his new life. His mom seemed to like having him there in the house with her—most of the time, anyway—and he was spending more time with his friends from church. Life was moving in a positive direction.

Now that Andrew was a free man, he wanted to be rebaptized—this time without the chains. Pastor Kieth agreed to rebaptize Andrew.

As Andrew stood in the baptismal tank at church with Pastor Kieth looking out over the sea of faces in his new church family, he could feel Pastor Kieth choosing his words carefully. Normally the pastor shared a short testimony with the church about the person he was baptizing, and Andrew had told him that he preferred not to share with everyone the fact that he'd been in prison. Andrew had to laugh when Pastor Kieth told everyone the same thing Andrew had told him when they'd first met—that he'd studied with Doug Batchelor, understood the tenets of the gospel, and he'd given his heart to God.

When Pastor Kieth dipped Andrew under the warm waters of the baptismal tank in the name of the Father, the Son, and the Holy Spirit,

Andrew came up soaking wet and smiling. John 8:36 was evident in his life in more ways than one: *So if the Son sets you free, you will indeed be free.*

In December 2005 Andrew received a package in the mail. It was wrapped in a shroud of layers, and the return address indicated it was from Todd, his last cellmate at McNeil Island, who had eventually forgiven him for the cookie crumbs and mess of tied socks and linens and was happy to hear that Andrew was doing well on the outside.

What in the world is this? Andrew wondered, peeling off the layers and layers of wrapping. Inside he found a ceramic crown. *Todd made this,* Andrew thought, smiling.

On the top of the crown was one word: "NO!" On the bottom of the crown an inscription read "From your favorite cellie in the whole world."

Andrew smiled as he looked at his ceramic crown. *The King of No,* he thought.

Chapter 24

As Andrew completed the last few classes he needed for his degree from Pierce College in the spring of 2006, he began to wonder if the University of Washington would accept him as a transfer student. He had gotten excellent grades, especially in his science, math, and engineering classes, and many of his teachers encouraged him to apply for the engineering program at UW. It seemed to be the logical choice to Andrew, too; after all, he had a background in mechanics and a certificate in welding, and he'd been studying calculus and physics. It would be a tidy educational progression, but the program was competitive, and he wasn't sure his transcripts measured up to the standard. Besides that, he hadn't worked a job since he left prison, and he had no idea how he was going to pay for college tuition if he did make it into the program.

As he had become accustomed to doing, Andrew asked God for guidance. *God,* he prayed, *I don't know if my grades are high enough to be accepted into the program or if I can even pay for it if I'm accepted. Please show me that You're still with me and still moving on my behalf.*

Andrew decided to proceed with the application process and see what God would do. As he filled out his application information and requested transcripts for his classes, however, there was one piece of the admissions puzzle that especially concerned him: his written personal statement.

I could write a great personal statement without ever mentioning where I've been, Andrew thought. *But should I?*

Andrew wrestled with the idea for a while, prayed about it, and finally made his decision. *No,* he decided. *I won't write a statement that excludes my time in prison. It's not me, and it leaves out God. I wouldn't even be here if it weren't for God.*

Andrew sat down and wrote everything. He shared about the low points in his life, his time in prison, as well as his emergence from the darkness when he'd met God. *They're getting the whole story,* Andrew thought as he sealed up the package and put it in the mail. *Maybe someone at the university needs to hear it.*

Two weeks later Andrew received a response—a letter on University of Washington letterhead requesting that Andrew meet with a woman from the administration office.

Andrew sat across the huge desk from the woman in the administration office, silently watching while she reviewed his application materials through the glasses settled on the bridge of her nose.

"Well," she said, scanning the pages in her hands. "You have great grades. Physics, chemistry, yes, good—all your prerequisites are out of the way." She paused for a moment and glanced up at him. "Two hundred fifty-four credits from Pierce College? OK, that's interesting."

Andrew shifted in his seat and smiled.

She turned through each page, and stopped when she reached Andrew's personal statement. He waited while she scanned through it. She looked up.

"You know," she said, "This is truly amazing. I've been working at this university for years, and we've never read a personal statement like this before—and neither have any of the professors or administrators." She put the stack of papers down on her desk and folded her hands on top of them. "As soon as everyone read your personal statement, you were admitted into UW hands down. And Andrew, there was no discussion—you are accepted into the engineering program. "

"Thank you," Andrew said. He breathed a sigh and let a smile take over his face.

"That's not all," the woman said. "I want to congratulate you on something else, too. You were given a full scholarship for as long as you're here."

Andrew stared at her in shock. "You mean . . .?"

"I mean, you have a full scholarship. Welcome to the engineering program at the University of Washington."

Andrew felt like dancing as he walked down the long hallway. *God, You are amazing!* he prayed as he glided down the steps and across the campus. *You gave me more than I even thought to ask for. I will do the best I can to honor You in everything I do. Everyone will know that I'm here because of You.*

Andrew graduated from Pierce College with honors and decided to pursue general classes through the summer before officially beginning the engineering program in the fall.

One afternoon as Andrew headed into the gym to work out, he saw a familiar face coming toward him through the doorway. Andrew stopped. It was a paradigm shift to see one of his prison friends on the street. It was Brandon from the work camp at McNeil. They'd fought fires together.

"Brandon!" Andrew said.

Brandon looked up. "Andrew! No way!"

They talked for a few minutes. Andrew was excited to find out that Brandon was also in school, pursuing a psychology degree. They exchanged contact information.

A few days later Andrew received an e-mail from Brandon. *Andrew,* it read, *Pierce College is looking for someone to be the keynote speaker at the McNeil Island graduation. I did it last year—I'm sure they'd love to have you speak. Are you interested?*

"Are you kidding me?" Andrew said out loud as he read the e-mail. The thought of going back to McNeil Island, this time as a free man, to tell his story, encourage the guys, and extend a ray of hope into that dark place from the outside—Andrew couldn't think of anything he wanted to do more. Within a few days he was scheduled to be the keynote speaker at the next McNeil Island graduation service.

In addition to the good news about his acceptance into the engineering program, the scholarship from the University of Washington, and the opportunity to speak at McNeil Island, Andrew had another reason to be excited. His mom had begun attending the Puyallup Seventh-day Adventist Church with him on Sabbath.

"Look, Andrew," his mom said one day after church. "One of my friends gave me this book. She says it's really good, so I'm going to read it."

"Let me see," Andrew said, "What is it?"

His mom held it up. "It's called *Faith That Works,* by Morris Venden."

Andrew couldn't believe it. "Mom, that's one of my favorite books! I read that entire book every single day for almost three years. You're going to love it."

"Well, we should study it together then," his mom suggested.

To Andrew's delight, he and his mom began reading *Faith That Works* and studying the Bible together every day for their devotional time with God. The book's message was just as powerful as Andrew remembered it, and his mom seemed to be enjoying it as well.

For the first time in Andrew's life, everything was headed in the right direction. His relationship with God was deep and satisfying, his social circle had expanded to include new quality friendships, and he was able to study and worship with his mom at home and at church. In addition, he had been accepted into the engineering program at the University of Washington on a full scholarship. Life felt as close to perfect as he could have imagined it.

And that's just exactly when everything started to go wrong.

★★★

Andrew's professor walked into the classroom, put his teaching materials down on the podium, and began writing on the board.

"The highest score on the thermodynamics quiz you took yesterday," Professor Rao announced to the class, scribbling on the board as he talked, "was an 83 percent. The average score was 65 percent. The lowest score in the class was 22 percent."

The class fell silent. Andrew was sure that if a bead of sweat dropped off his forehead, the whole class would hear it splash on the floor. *Everybody's wondering who the idiot is,* Andrew thought grimly. They didn't have to wait long to find out.

The professor put the chalk down on the tray, turned around, and pointed at Andrew. "Mr. Michell," he said. "I want to see you after class."

Andrew's face burned as the other students turned to look at him. *What is happening to me?* Andrew thought. *When did my brain shrivel into a raisin?*

Andrew waited after class for the other students to leave, and then he made his way down to the podium where the professor was gathering his teaching materials. When the professor handed him his quiz paper, Andrew stared at it in defeat. There was so much red ink that the pages looked as if they were bleeding. He had failed. Again.

"Why did this happen?" Professor Rao asked. "What's the problem?"

Andrew shook his head. He honestly didn't know. A few weeks into class something had gone wrong. His mind had gone completely blank. At the end of each lecture he would walk out and not remember anything he had heard. He studied, but couldn't remember anything he had read. He had failed every assignment, every quiz, and every test. His professors were surprised, but no one was more surprised than Andrew. He had never failed anything before in his entire life.

Andrew looked up at his professor. "I have no idea what's wrong," he said. "I just don't know. But I'll make a deal with you. If I don't get an *A* on your next quiz, I'll drop your class. Does that make it easy?"

"That makes it really easy," the professor said, studying him. "That's fine."

God, I don't understand, Andrew said silently as he walked away from his puzzled-looking professor. *After all these years of reading everything I could get my hands on, after learning all the trades available, after getting straight A's in all the college classes I took while in prison, after wowing the committee with my essay and getting accepted in the UW engineering program, after graduating from Pierce College with honors, suddenly I'm . . . failing? How is this even possible? What's happening?*

Even before he left the classroom, Andrew felt it deep in his core—his future in engineering was over.

During the next few weeks his college counselor, his professors, and his mom tried to convince him to continue on. Maybe he just needed to see a therapist. Maybe he just needed a short break—he'd been studying nonstop since he was 16 years old, after all. Maybe his brain was just tired. But for Andrew, all of the worst fears he'd had in prison were being realized.

Here it is, Andrew thought, lying on his bed staring at the wall. *This is the evidence that I'm never really going to make it. It may appear on the surface to some people that I'm going to do something or go somewhere or be somebody, but it's not real. Here I am. And I'm failing.*

Andrew thought about Frank O'Dell from Green Hill telling him he expected Andrew to do great things when he got out of prison. He thought about Joseph Smyly driving all the way to Olympia on his own time to testify before the clemency board that Andrew should be given the opportunity to prove himself outside the prison. He thought of Governor Gary Locke signing his name to the document that set Andrew free. He thought of his mom, Jeremy, and all of his friends from church, and the committee at the University of Washington that accepted him into the engineering program and gave him a full scholarship—all expecting him to succeed. He was letting them all down. He was letting himself down. Worst of all, he was letting God down.

All of Andrew's classmates knew he was a Sabbathkeeping Christian who didn't drink or party and ate a vegetarian diet. Instead of being like Daniel in the Bible and succeeding beyond his peers who weren't Christians and didn't take care of their bodies, he was falling far behind them. And instead of being drawn to the Jesus in Andrew, his classmates all thought he was weird. And now, on top of it all, he was failing, failing, failing. Such an enormous opportunity to glorify God . . . lost in a barrage of failing grades.

Despite everything Andrew had been through, this was the lowest moment of his life. It bothered him that he was failing, but the greatest pain he felt was failing God. His successes glorified God. But his failures couldn't possibly glorify God, could they?

The semester ended, and Andrew fell into despair. His life was spiraling downward into insignificance. He didn't know how to go about planning for the future or what to do now that there was a huge blockade on the path he had chosen. He lost confidence in his own ability to make decisions. *So this is what it feels like to be shaken to the core,* he thought. He was losing control of his life, and losing control of himself.

Chapter 25

Andrew was in a foul mood when he woke up Sunday morning. In addition to the stress he felt about his failure in school, he and his mom hadn't been getting along, and the tension was mounting.

Their argument had started over something simple, but it ended with Andrew slamming his fist down on the kitchen table. He hadn't lost his temper in years, but now, here at home in a standoff with his mom, he'd given in to a moment of anger that left his fist throbbing and his mom frozen with a fearful expression. When he saw the look of terror in his mother's eyes, guilt and frustration washed over him.

"I'm going for a drive," Andrew said. He picked the truck keys up off the counter and left his mom standing in the kitchen. "I've got to get some air."

I'll go visit Jeremy and Christina for a while, Andrew thought, turning the keys in the ignition and trying to swallow the old familiar rage that clawed his throat. *Maybe spending some time with friends from church will help me cool off.*

As he drove down Canyon Road toward Jeremy and Christina's apartment, Andrew gripped the steering wheel tightly. He hated the rage that still boiled inside him. When he had become a Christian, God had given him victory and healing in a lot of areas of his life. But there were obviously still areas of his life that were not under control—issues that God hadn't solved yet. And in Andrew's estimation, God had been unusually quiet during the past several months since he'd been home.

Andrew clenched his teeth together. *Where is the fulfillment of promises? How can I tell people that Jesus saves when I'm still dealing with not being perfect and making mistakes and feeling self-destructive? Where is the confidence? Where is the victory? Is God really strong enough to save me?*

As those thoughts took root in Andrew's mind, the anger inside him grew. He pounded the steering wheel with his hands. *What is happening to* me? What is happening to my life? Where did God go? he thought bitterly. Up ahead, the stoplight on 128th Street turned yellow, and in that moment a dark thought formed in his mind.

Stop, he thought. Apply the brake and stop.

Punch it, a voice said. Put the gas pedal down on the floorboard and gun it. What difference does it make? What purpose do you have now, anyway? You can't make it out here. Prison messed you up, and now you're a failure.

There was a seed of common sense in Andrew's mind that told him he shouldn't even consider doing what he was about to do; but the dark thought took over, and Andrew felt as though he were outside of himself, watching. Instead of applying the brake, Andrew jammed the gas pedal all the way down to the floor. The speedometer needle steadily climbed from 40 miles per hour, to 60, to 80.

The light turned red, and the speedometer crept up to 90. The light had already been red for three or four seconds when Andrew plunged through the busy intersection at 90 miles per hour. He should have crashed into cross traffic, but for some reason none of the cross traffic had entered the intersection yet.

As he left the intersection and saw cars begin to cross behind him in his rearview mirror, Andrew came back to himself and nearly collapsed, barely hanging onto the steering wheel as he braked and pulled over to the side of the road. I can't believe I just did something so stupid, he said to himself. I just did something ridiculous and self-destructive that could have hurt other people, too.

His hands were shaking as he sat on the side of the road. The anger had washed out of him, like the receding waters of a tsunami wave. Andrew could hear his friend Matthew from prison in his mind, saying, "Andrew, it feels as though there's an intelligent force in my life that is trying to destroy me."

God, Andrew prayed, I need You now more than ever. I should know by now that I can't control myself. I need You to take my will. There are unholy things in my life that are still clinging to me. I am confused about my future. Please don't let go of me. Don't take Your Holy Spirit away from me. Please help me.

Andrew was not himself when he got to Jeremy and Christina's house. He didn't tell them about his experience at the intersection—he was too ashamed to admit he'd done that. They invited him in as usual, and Andrew sat on the couch.

As he talked with Jeremy, Andrew leaned forward and clasped his hands together. "Jeremy," he said, "tell me something. You know how all my plans for school have fallen apart. I don't know which direction I'm supposed to go. So how do I know what God's will is?"

Jeremy nodded his head thoughtfully before he spoke. "You know, Andrew, I spent a year in Lithuania as a student missionary. My experience there taught me a lot, and while I don't know exactly what God has planned for you, I do know that it is *always* God's will to reach people who don't know about Him. No matter what you do, that will *always* be God's will."

Andrew let that idea percolate in his mind on his way home. When he got back to the house, he apologized to his mom for his outburst, and then went to his room to spend some time by himself.

God, You're still there, right? Andrew prayed. He waited, hoping for some indication of God's presence. *You promised You would never leave me or forsake me. It's right here,* Andrew continued, thumping his Bible emphatically. Andrew's hopes fell. No crashing thunder, no jagged strike of lightning. Not even a still small voice.

Discouraged, Andrew opened his Bible and began to read some of the promises he'd underlined during his years of study in prison, hoping that some of them would penetrate the sour candy shell forming around his heart.

Jeremiah 29:11: "'For I know the plans I have for you,' says the Lord. 'They are plans for good and not for disaster, to give you a future and a hope.'"

How is failing my college classes a plan for good? Andrew wondered. *It doesn't make sense.*

As Andrew reviewed some of his favorite stories and verses, however, he noticed a pattern. David had fasted and prayed when his child had been sick. Esther had fasted and prayed when her people had been on the brink of death. Daniel had fasted and prayed when he'd had a disturbing vision he didn't understand. Each of these people had faced a serious, unknown future. And each one of them had fasted and prayed to God.

I know there is a relationship between spirituality and food, Andrew thought. He had fasted and prayed before while he was still in prison. *But maybe fasting is a spiritual discipline I need to take more seriously,* he told himself.

Andrew flipped the pages of his Bible until he came to Matthew 6:16, where Jesus talked about fasting: *"And when you fast,'* Andrew read, *"don't make it obvious, as the hypocrites do, who try to look pale and disheveled so people will admire them for their fasting. I assure you, that is the only reward they will ever get. But when you fast, comb your hair and wash your face. Then no one will suspect you are fasting, except your Father, who knows what you do in secret. And your Father, who knows all secrets, will reward you."*

H'mmm, Andrew thought. *Jesus said, "When you fast," not "If you fast."*

Andrew remembered something else, too—a quote he had read in the book *Counsels on Diet and Foods* in prison. He thumbed through the book until he found it: "For certain things, fasting and prayer are recommended and appropriate. In the hand of God they are a means of cleansing the heart and promoting a receptive frame of mind. We obtain answers to our prayers because we humble our souls before God" (pp. 187, 188).

That's what I need, Andrew thought. *A clean heart and a receptive frame of mind.*

For the next 21 days Andrew fasted and prayed, begging God to open his heart and mind and show him what to do. Each day he wrote in his journal, emptying his mind of everything and pouring it out onto the paper before God. The experience was intense, but at the end of his fast he still had not received any firm revelations.

Andrew ate normally for a week, and then began another fast. *What if God has already shown me what to do, and I'm just not getting it?* Andrew thought. He continued to pray and write in his journal. Some of it was just fluff—nonsensical things he wrote down anyway. He remembered things he'd written in his journal during his time in prison—silly hopes and dreams, such as "someday I'm going to go to Venezuela," and "Sometime I plan to go to Thailand."

On the last Thursday night of his second fast Andrew fell asleep but woke up in the middle of the night. He looked over at the clock. It was 3:00 a.m. He closed his eyes and turned over.

Suddenly he felt as though he were being chased. He turned around and saw huge, colorful dragons chasing him. His heart pounded, and he wanted to run, but his legs wouldn't move. As they neared him, however, he noticed that they were becoming bloated and sick, and their tongues were hanging out of their mouths.

Look ahead, a voice said to Andrew. Andrew turned and saw Jesus. He was wearing a robe and sandals, and he was jumping up and down like an excited parent during a kids' soccer game. "Yes!" Jesus said, cheering. "Andrew is serious! He's fasting!"

The connection between food and spirituality is huge, the voice said. This time, the voice boomed and echoed in his head.

The images evaporated from Andrew's mind and the sound of the echoing voice faded. *Was I dreaming?* he wondered, his heart still pounding. *That was so bizarre.*

Andrew closed his eyes again, and drifted off to sleep. When he woke up, the vision of Jesus cheering him on was still vivid in his mind. He wrote it down in his journal and thought about it several times during the day.

That night, as Andrew lay in bed, the thought occurred to him: *Look into your mind again.* As Andrew closed his eyes and turned to look, he realized that the dragons were gone, and in their place was a pile of bones—skeletons of the dragons that had been chasing him.

Wow! Andrew thought. *That's incredible.*

The next morning Andrew awoke and turned on his light. He rolled over and opened his Bible, and as he did, the thought again occurred to him: *Look in the rearview mirror of your mind and see what you can see now.*

Andrew lay back down on his pillow and closed his eyes. This time when he looked behind him, there was nothing except dust being blown away by the wind. *What does it mean?* Andrew wondered. He knew that God sometimes communicated with people through dreams and visions, but Andrew couldn't make sense of what he'd seen.

It was the final day of his fast, and Andrew still didn't understand. *God, what are You trying to tell me?* Andrew asked. *What is it that was chasing me, but is now crumbled to dust because of my time fasting and praying to You?*

Dragon bones, a thundering voice, and Jesus cheering him on? Andrew was more confused than ever.

Chapter 26

Andrew was still feeling depressed and directionless when he found out that Pastor William was planning to take a mission team with him to conduct a Vacation Bible School for the children of La Paz, Mexico.

The idea of sharing God with kids in Mexico intrigued Andrew, and when Pastor William asked him to be part of the group, he decided to go.

"My Spanish isn't very good," Andrew warned Pastor William.

Pastor William laughed. "In Mexico you don't have to speak Spanish to reach the kids. If you know how to hang upside down on a swing set and play soccer in the street, you're in."

Well, Andrew thought, *at least by helping with a mission project I'll be doing something significant with my time while I wait for God to show me what He wants for my life.*

La Paz was beautiful, and Andrew was amazed at the stunning rock cliffs overlooking an ocean that sparkled in varying shades of azure. He loved the warm, salty breezes, the array of fresh fruits they had to eat, and the fascinating culture. He was glad he'd taken Spanish classes at Pierce College, and as he communicated haltingly with the kids, he found he had retained more of the language than he had thought.

More than anything, though, Andrew felt a deep sense of satisfaction when he looked into the deep-brown eyes of the kids and watched the looks on their faces when they heard stories about God and people in the Bible. Andrew knew what it felt like to be captured and enthralled with a new understanding of God, and in some ways he felt as if he were discovering it all over again with the kids.

As his time in Mexico drew to a close, Andrew hated to see it end. He'd been thinking about it while he was there, and something from his journals stirred in his mind. "I want to do more of this," Andrew told Pastor William. "You wouldn't happen to know of any mission opportunities in Venezuela, would you?"

"Actually," Pastor William said, "I do. There's a team of students from

Atlantic Union College that is going to Venezuela to do a church building project. I'm sure they would love to have your help."

Back at home Andrew made preparations to go to Venezuela. He looked forward to being part of a mission team again, but his heart was still heavy. People he knew from church were asking him questions about how school was going and where he was headed. He told them all the same thing—that he was taking a break from school and doing some mission work. He couldn't bear to let them know he'd failed school, failed himself, and failed God. Each time someone asked, Andrew felt worse.

In addition, someone from Amazing Facts had heard the story about how he'd been able to study the Bible in prison along with the *Bible Answers Live* program, and they wanted to write an article about him.

Again Andrew fasted and prayed. *God, please,* he begged. *Show me what I'm supposed to be doing with my life. People keep asking me about my future. I'm so afraid that if people see me fail, they'll question Your faithfulness, and all I've ever wanted to do is honor You. I don't want to let You down. Please don't let me embarrass You.*

At the end of his fast Andrew felt even more discouraged. He was supposed to leave for Venezuela soon, and he'd heard nothing from God. No handwriting on the wall. No voice from the sky. No path of dry land between parted seas.

And in the midst of it all, Andrew had to go back to prison.

When Andrew had agreed to speak for the Pierce College commencement ceremonies back at the McNeil Island Corrections Center, everything in his life had been wonderful. He was in school, he was doing well, he was spiritually charged, and he was optimistic. He couldn't wait to go back to the prison and share the message of hope that was lighting him from the inside out.

Now, as he stood on the dock and watched the McNeil Island ferry chugging toward him across the choppy water, he felt anticipation and dread battling for supremacy inside his mind as he prepared to go back inside the prison. He looked out toward the island, where the tower kept watch over the whitewashed institution he had called home for so many years. He had been free for two years. And all he had to show for it was an associate's degree and some pictures of kids in Mexico.

In the chapel Andrew sat with the other college officials. Staring back at him were inmates who were graduating with their GED or their welding certificate or some other mark of achievement.

A few years ago I was sitting there, Andrew thought. *I know exactly what's going through their minds: Let's get this ceremony done so we can have cake and ice cream.* An event such as this was the only time the prisoners could have real cake and ice cream.

The warden got up to speak, then a number of college officials spoke. Finally it was Andrew's turn. When he was introduced and stood up to the podium, he saw recognition in their faces, and he heard a chorus of whispers spread through the crowd of prisoners.

"That guy looks familiar," Andrew heard one guy say, nudging the person next to him.

"Man," one inmate said to another, "is that *Andy?*"

Andrew looked out over the familiar faces, and when he did, he knew exactly what they needed, because he'd been there. They needed hope. He told his story of going to prison and finding God. He told them about his clemency, and how important his education had been in the process. He told them about his scholarship to the University of Washington, and how he'd just gotten back from Mexico. For 10 minutes he talked to the guys as friends and tried to encourage them.

"And tomorrow morning," Andrew said, "I'm on a plane to Venezuela to help with a church building project there."

The guys cheered for him as though he were a returning hero—someone who had survived their nightmare and managed to make it in the world outside of the razor-wired fences. He could see it in their faces—he had inspired them. It should have felt good. But inside Andrew was hurting. He was telling them only the good stuff, not the failures—that aspect of his life was too painful to share. Afterward, as he shook their hands and saw the tears in their eyes when they thanked him, Andrew felt like a big fat hypocrite.

As Andrew left the prison he continued to wrestle with the mixed emotions he felt about the direction of his life. Although he did not know the path God wanted him to take, for the next month Andrew would be working in Venezuela.

The mission experience in Venezuela was everything Andrew had hoped it would be. It felt good to be doing something that was productive for God. It was the same feeling he'd had when he was in Mexico—a feeling that felt a lot like . . . *significance.*

He didn't want to let go of that feeling, but he knew that all too soon his time in Venezuela would draw to a close and he would be back home in Washington without a plan. *What does God have in mind for my life?* Andrew wondered.

"Look, Andrew!" his mom said when he arrived home. "It's the Amazing Facts article they wrote about you!"

Andrew took the paper in her hand and looked at the article. There was a picture of him speaking to the prisoners at the McNeil Island graduation ceremony, and just below it there was another picture of him posing with two of the little kids from his Mexico trip, a big grin plastered across his face. He stared at the picture for a long time, and couldn't help smiling as he remembered playing with them and singing songs with them about God.

I've got to go again, Andrew thought.

That November Pastor Kieth asked Andrew for a favor. "Andrew, would you be willing to share your story with the pastors at our next regional pastors' meeting?"

Andrew swallowed. "In front of a room full of pastors?"

"Yes," Pastor Kieth said.

"Uh . . ." Andrew thought for a minute. Except for talking to the prisoners in the familiar chapel at McNeil Island, he'd never done any public speaking, and the thought of standing in front of a sea of unfamiliar faces made his insides turn to ice. His own church family hadn't even heard his story. Most of them didn't know he'd ever been to prison. When they asked about his past, he told them he used to be a welder and firefighter, and now he'd moved home to live with his mom and go to school. He just left out the detail about welding and firefighting in prison. "I guess . . . I guess I could," he managed to say.

When Andrew walked into the room full of pastors, however, he wondered what he'd gotten himself into. *Oh, no,* he thought. *What on earth am I going to say? I've never done this before, and all these guys are professional speakers.*

Andrew sat down next to Pastor Kieth and rubbed his fingers together nervously. *Bad idea,* he thought. *Why did I ever agree to speak in public?* At least he wasn't the first speaker. He was so nervous that he had to clench his teeth to keep them from chattering.

At the beginning of the meeting the leader gave handouts to each of the pastors. Since he was in the room, Andrew received the stack of papers as well. One of the handouts was a magazine, and Andrew began to thumb through it. When he saw the featured article, he stopped and stared. *No way,* he thought.

The article was titled "Basic Tips on Public Speaking."

Andrew quickly read the article and took notes. He had just finished reading the article when Elder Freedman got up and introduced Andrew as their next speaker.

Andrew stood up and walked to the front. He turned to face the audience of pastors and swallowed hard. "Well, I've never spoken publicly before, and I don't know how to speak well," Andrew said, holding up the magazine handout, "but for the past half hour I've been reading this article with tips on public speaking, so I think it's going to be OK."

The pastors all laughed, and Andrew relaxed a little bit. He started talking, his story falling out in disjointed pieces. When he finished, he noticed that some of the pastors were emotional. *I guess it must not have been that bad,* he thought.

"You did fine," Pastor Kieth encouraged him when he was done.

"It was a little disjointed," Andrew whispered.

"Listen," Pastor Kieth said, "this is a tough crowd. I could tell in the beginning, they weren't really interested—they probably thought it was just another testimony about a con who had found Jesus. But take a look around. These pastors felt the power of God in your testimony."

Andrew wasn't sure why anyone would want to hear his story. And frankly, he'd been embarrassed to tell it. Who would want to stand up in front of a group of people and talk about all of their bad life choices and their time in prison?

And yet this was the second time Andrew had seen people respond to God through his story. And if God could be honored through his failures and mistakes, then it was worth it.

Chapter 27

Andrew stood in the Stafford Creek Corrections Center parking lot and leaned up against the truck. It was usual weather for January in the Northwest—cold and wet—but Andrew didn't care. Any minute now those big glass doors would open, and Brian would come walking out.

Andrew hadn't seen Brian in more than three years, though they had talked on the phone several times. Brian—the guy who always seemed to be a few cells down from Andrew, no matter which institution he was in. Brian—the guy who convinced him to get rid of his Danzig album. Brian—the guy Andrew interviewed for Mr. Mohrbacher's English class. He couldn't wait to see him.

Brian had been in prison for 17 long years. The day he went to jail, Andrew guessed, he probably had a hundred friends. But, as Andrew also knew from experience, the day of his release, he would be lucky to have one or two. Andrew was glad to be there for his friend.

That's what happens when you pass the years away behind prison bars, Andrew thought. *People don't care. People forget you.*

When the glass doors opened and Brian came walking out, they greeted each other like long-lost brothers. When they got into the truck and Andrew started the ignition, he looked over at Brian in the passenger's seat. He had to smile as he remembered his own ride home from prison.

"Hang on," Andrew said, grinning. "You're going to feel like a martian for a while. Trust me. It's normal."

On the way home they stopped at the lake house in Olympia and took a picture to commemorate the first day of the rest of Brian's life.

★★★

Andrew stood up in front of his church family on Sabbath morning. He was finally ready to tell everyone a story he knew would shock many of the people he'd been attending church with for more than three years. As the story of his life as a troubled teenager and then as a convicted felon fell from his lips, he could see the looks of surprise on several faces. They laughed with him, and some of them were moved to tears. But when he was finished, everyone embraced him the same way they had nearly three years ago when he'd first met them—openly, without judgment.

"You guys have shown me so much love," Andrew said, looking out over the faces.

After that, Andrew was invited to share his story at other churches, and he found that his weekends were almost always filled with speaking engagements. Some people accepted him and were amazed at what God had done with his life, but some people didn't approve. They called it pride. They called it glorifying sin. They called it benefiting from his crimes. Andrew was stunned.

How can they think I like telling people I'm an ex-con? Andrew wondered. *That's not something that makes me proud. It makes me ashamed. The only thing I can possibly brag about is what the apostle Paul bragged about—what happened on the cross and how Jesus saved me. That's it.*

One Sabbath, after telling his testimony as a guest speaker at another church, he was riding home with his friend Jeremy. Their trip would take them a couple of hours, and they had plenty of time to talk as the miles of yellow lines passed.

"I'm telling my testimony every weekend, I'm doing mission trips. I just wish I knew what God wanted me to do with my life," Andrew said. "Jeremy, tell me something. How do I know what God's will is for me?"

Jeremy looked over at Andrew. "All I can tell you is that it's always God's will to do mission work. It's always God's will to reach the unreached. It's always God's will to take the message of hope to people who have never heard it before."

Suddenly Andrew understood. *How could I have missed it?* he wondered. *The answer has been there the whole time.* It was as if he was looking into a giant kaleidoscope, and every particle was perfectly in focus for the first time.

A few days before, Andrew had read a quote by Oswald Smith: "No one has the right to hear the gospel twice, while there remains someone who has not heard it once." Now, riding in the car, he'd heard the same sentiment echoed in Jeremy's words. Realization unfolded inside Andrew, and he became more excited as every second passed. The dreams he'd had in his heart since he was in prison—dreams of going to Venezuela, Thailand, and other places in the world—God had planted them there on purpose.

Andrew grinned as he stared ahead at the road. "Jeremy, I've known you for three years. How many times do you suppose I've asked you that question?"

"Probably 10 times," Jeremy said. "And I've given you the same answer every time."

Andrew nodded. "You're right. But this is the first time I've really heard you. I know what God's will is for my life." It made all the sense in the world.

From that moment, Andrew felt a new surge of energy and enthusiasm for life. He started reading mission books, he researched mission opportunities, and he studied his Bible with a new enthusiasm. His purpose was clear, and he couldn't wait to get started.

A few weeks later he found out that a girl from church was planning to attend a new lay evangelism institute in Orlando, Florida.

"It's four months of intensive training," she told him. "They offer all kinds of classes on Bible topics and outreach and missionary work. After the four months they're sending students on a six-month missionary project in Thailand."

Thailand! Andrew thought. *No way!*

It wasn't a lightning strike or handwriting on the wall. It was better. It was Thailand!

Andrew poured himself into every moment he spent at the lay evangelism institute. He felt like himself again, studying and absorbing the material with a sharp mind, hungry to learn everything he could in preparation for his mission.

While Andrew was in Orlando, he met Pastor Derek Morris and his wife, Bodil, at the Forest Lake Seventh-day Adventist Church. He discovered that they were part of a singing group called Trilogy, which arranged verses from the Bible and sang them word for word over beautiful contemporary music arrangements. Andrew enjoyed the songs, partly because they were simple scripture, and partly because they were soothing and helped him feel closer to God.

What a leap to go from Danzig to scripture songs, Andrew laughed to himself. But music was such a huge part of his life before he became a Christian, and he was thankful to have found Christian music he enjoyed.

When the time came to go to Thailand, Andrew was ready. As he had hoped, Thailand was amazing and strange and wonderful. Andrew loved the people, and he began to learn the language and study the culture. He was fascinated with all of it—the beautiful shimmering beaches, the crowded markets, and the animal sanctuaries. More than anything, he wanted to introduce the people of Thailand to the God who had changed his life.

One after another, opportunities began to open up for Andrew to share God. Empowered by God's obvious leading and a sense of purpose,

Andrew engaged himself 100 percent. There was something about fulfilling his mission there that actually fulfilled *him*. He felt it when he taught students at the local Buddhist high school, when he spoke at a youth event at the university, and when he preached about the Bible at camp meetings.

And yet, as his six-month commitment in Thailand neared an end, Andrew felt torn. He loved serving the people of Thailand, but he felt a distinct impression that for some unknown reason he had to leave.

It was a few days before his flight was scheduled to take him back to the United States that Andrew began feeling homesick for the beautiful countryside and lovely people of Thailand that he hadn't even left yet. Afternoon melted into evening, and Andrew found himself sitting on a covered porch at the home of an old Thai farmer named Somchai.

Somchai's house was perched on the very top of a small hill, overlooking his farm below, with a lush backdrop of rolling green hills beyond. Andrew sat on the veranda, swatting pesky mosquitoes and chatting with Somchai about his impending trip. They both knew Andrew didn't want to leave.

"What are you going to do?" Somchai asked.

"I don't know," Andrew admitted. "I'm not really sure. But I feel that I need to go home."

Somchai was adamant. "You cannot leave here, Andrew. You need to stay here. The youth here need you. The people in the community need you. Asia needs you. People here don't have hope of eternal life as you do. Nobody here knows a God that can transform lives as your God can. The youth have no foundation for hope, and they need your example."

Andrew swallowed hard as he listened.

"Do not go home," Somchai pleaded. "Please stay here. If you go, who will share with them?"

Andrew felt that Somchai's words were an affirmation of his ministry in Thailand. He knew he belonged in missions. It was the ultimate confirmation he needed to know that God *had* brought him here to fulfill a purpose. It was hard to have to say goodbye when there was so much of God's work left to do. Here Somchai was begging him to live as a Christian among people who didn't know God. How could he possibly refuse? And yet . . .

"Somchai, I don't know why," Andrew said, "but I have to go. I feel it. I'm supposed to go."

As they sat on the porch soaking up the sunset, Andrew made a promise. "God willing, Somchai, when I've completed whatever it is He wants me to do somewhere else, I'll return to Thailand."

Reluctantly, a few days later Andrew packed his bags, got onto the plane, and headed back to the United States.

After the long flight he was grateful to be back on solid ground and headed home for some rest. He entered the familiar front door to his home and set his bags down on the floor. Just then the phone rang.

It was Erik, a friend he'd made while at the lay evangelism institute. Erik was a former marijuana-smoking snowboard instructor who divided his time between Colorado and Argentina to take advantage of snowboard season in both hemispheres. He'd given his life to God, and their paths had crossed in Orlando.

"Hey," Erik said. "What are you doing? I just found out that there's a need for teachers at a school in Costa Rica. It's a six-month assignment, and I'm going. They need one more person to teach Bible and English. Can you go too?"

Andrew laughed. "I literally just got off a plane from Thailand."

"So . . . you can come?" Erik asked.

The next few days were a whirlwind of activity as Andrew prepared to embark on another adventure in a different country. Before he knew it, he was dusting off his Spanish-speaking skills and stepping off a plane in the jungles of Costa Rica.

Chapter 28

Her fingernails were black, her clothing was black, and her mood was as dark as nightfall deep in the jungle.

Andrew sat at his desk next to the chalkboard watching the students in his class. They were all busily working on their assignments. That is, all except one—Maria continually perplexed him.

What am I going to do with you? Andrew wondered, tapping his fingers silently on the desk.

Even now as he watched, Maria sat in the back row carving a skull into her desk. Since the beginning of the school year a few months earlier, she had sullenly refused to do her homework, and when Andrew asked for her completed assignments, she unloaded a few volatile sentences on him through curled, sneering lips. His Spanish wasn't fantastic, but he was fluent enough to know that she was calling him choice names and swearing at him. A couple of times she had threatened to commit suicide, and Andrew was concerned. Her odd behavior wasn't reserved exclusively for Andrew's class, either; she was regularly in trouble with all of the teachers, and spent almost as much time in the hall and in the principal's office as she did in class.

Though Andrew liked to joke around and have fun with the kids outside of school hours, he was strict in the classroom. His class rules protected the learning environment so that the students who wanted a solid understanding of the material could obtain it without distraction. Most of the kids did well; Maria did not.

Class ended, and Andrew sat in the room alone after the kids left, thinking as he stared out the window at rich, tropical foliage and brightly colored birds. It wasn't *that* long ago that he had been the student all the teachers dreaded; he'd been the problem child, and no one could get through to him because he wouldn't let anyone in.

As he pondered how to help Maria, his mind wandered back to memories of his sixth-grade teacher, Mrs. Ammon, who had taught him during his last year in elementary school. That year he was constantly bored. He'd sit at his desk feeling imprisoned in his own skin while the fluorescent lights hummed above him and Mrs. Ammon's chalk scratched away at the chalkboard. He never paid attention to her lectures, and he never turned in his homework, although he would generally get 100 percent on his tests—an irony that apparently both pleased and perturbed Mrs. Ammon's sensibilities.

Andrew's favorite school days were the ones during which Mrs. Ammon was gone and there was a substitute teacher. Andrew would open the latch to the window just enough so it didn't click, and when the substitute teacher went to lunch, he would sneak back in through the window and change the grades on the computer or steal the teacher's editions of the textbooks.

One day when Mrs. Ammon came back from being gone, she was armed with a report from the substitute teacher that, of course, had Andrew's name on it. Andrew had poured paint into the huge classroom dictionary so the pages stuck together. He didn't know why he'd done it; it had just seemed like a funny thing to do at the time.

"Andrew," she said sweetly, "I'd like to see you after class, please."

Andrew had smirked and slid back in his seat. He watched as the other kids stuffed their papers and books into their backpacks and headed for the buses. Mrs. Ammon waited several minutes until all the students had gone, and the teachers had packed up their things and left for the day. When it was silent, she finally came over to him. "Let's go outside," she said.

Mrs. Ammon had led him out of the classroom exit and away from the school. When they arrived at some trees and bushes on the edge of the grounds where no one could see them, she stuck her bony finger in his face and transformed into a foulmouthed, monster lunatic before Andrew's very eyes. She must have bottled up every moment of her anger and frustration and saved it for the precise time when there was no one else around and she could tell Andrew exactly what she thought of him. And she did.

Mrs. Ammon ranted for several minutes, screaming at him through clenched teeth. Spit came out of her mouth along with words Andrew had never heard before as she described how much she hated him and what she thought of him. He was normally a pretty brazen and unaffected kid, but Mrs. Ammon's unleashed wrath was even more than he could stand, and he cried. No one had ever talked to him like that before. He never told anybody about Mrs. Ammon's verbal deluge; he figured no one would ever believe it. And even if they did, no one would have blamed her for what she said.

But her tirade didn't change Andrew's behavior in class. The incident actually gave him new motivation to make Mrs. Ammon's life miserable.

He wouldn't have been surprised if she'd retired the next year solely because of him.

Andrew didn't believe in karma, but he was pretty sure that if he did, his belief would include being repaid for his misbehavior as a child by Maria. Unlike Mrs. Ammon, however, Andrew didn't feel rage or anger toward Maria and her defiant behavior. Come to think of it, he hadn't felt that dark surge of rage in a long time. *Maybe that was one of the "dragons" put to death during my fast,* Andrew thought. Instead of anger, he felt concern for Maria beyond her scholastic decline. He could see that there was a spiritual battle raging inside this angry teenage girl.

"Let's start praying specifically for Maria," Andrew told Erik one morning when they met for prayer. They'd been meeting since the beginning of the school year at 4:30 in the morning to start their day talking to God and spending time in His presence. While they always prayed for their students in general, their main focus lately was asking God for wisdom on how to reach the community beyond the school.

Now Andrew wanted to include Maria as a special focus during their time with God. "Something is going on with her," Andrew explained to Erik. "I just feel unsettled, as though it's urgent that we pray consistently for her."

Erik agreed, and they began to pray for Maria every morning. In contrast to their expectations, however, the more they prayed for Maria, the worse she behaved. She became even more violent and angry, and she spared no energy in making Andrew's teaching job difficult.

"What's going on?" Andrew wondered out loud to Erik one morning while they prayed. "The situation should be getting better, not worse."

Erik was baffled as well. "I don't know, man," he said. "We'll just have to keep praying harder and see what happens."

Something else had also been on Andrew's mind for the past several mornings during their prayer time. They had been asking God for a way to reach outside the boundaries of the school with the good news about the life-changing power of God, and an idea had come into Andrew's mind. It was a far-fetched idea, though, and he hesitated to share it with Erik. Each morning as they prayed, the idea came to him more and more forcefully.

After several mornings of resisting the idea, Andrew finally decided to tell Erik about it. *If he thinks it's crazy, then I can finally let it rest,* Andrew thought.

"What do you think," Andrew said hesitantly when they met to pray, "about going to the local television or radio station and telling them my story?"

Erik looked up. "You mean, about how you went to prison and God changed your life?"

"Yes," Andrew said, feeling doubtful even as the words came out of his mouth. "I just can't get the idea out of my head. My story is embarrassing to me, but if it can get God some airtime in the local community, then maybe it's worth telling."

"Of course!" Erik said. Andrew could see him getting increasingly excited as the thought germinated in Erik's mind. "Why didn't we think of this sooner? It's a great idea! We've been asking God for a way to spread the message in the community, and I think this might be it."

With Erik's affirmation, Andrew agreed to contact the local radio and television stations. Within a few days a television reporter and a camera crew from channel 11 news showed up at the school. They interviewed Andrew, took some footage of him with his class, and asked Erik some questions on camera before they packed up and left.

"Well," Andrew asked Erik, "how do you think it went?"

"Great," Erik said. "You were able to really emphasize how God has changed your life. It's going to be powerful."

"I hope so," Andrew said.

A few days later Andrew was in his classroom preparing for his next class when he heard screaming and a commotion coming from down the hall. *What in the world is going on?* he wondered, putting his books down and walking toward the door.

A crowd of kids was gathering in the hallway looking at something that Andrew could not see. "What's happening?" Andrew asked, stopping some kids who were running toward him from the crowd. "What's going on? Who is over there?"

The kids looked at him with wide eyes, and one of them answered. "It is Maria, *Profe!*" he said. *Profe* was the nickname the kids had given him, short for the Spanish word *professor,* meaning "teacher."

Andrew felt his heart drop, and he put his hand on the boy's shoulder. "What about Maria?" he asked. "What happened? Tell me!"

"It is bad, *Profe,*" the boy said, trying not to cry. "Maria . . . Maria slit her wrists!"

Andrew let go of the boy's shoulder and ran down the hall, pushing past the kids. *Please, God,* he prayed. *Please let her be all right.*

Chapter 29

Andrew stood in front of the mirror looking at the scar on his stomach. It was a constant reminder of the detrimental path he had been on when at 16 he'd sliced himself with scissors the night he'd fought with his dad. He ran his thumb across the raised scar. A lot of years had passed since then, but the memory of his past would always be there. All the self-destructive rage that had motivated Maria to cut her own wrists—he knew it by heart. He'd lived it.

And now Maria will live with her own self-inflicted scars, Andrew thought, shaking his head sadly. But at least she would live. He was thankful for that.

God, Andrew prayed, *Erik and I have been praying for Maria for weeks now. We've asked again and again for You to intervene in her life like You did in ours. Why did this happen? You've promised in the Bible that if I pray earnestly, there will be powerful results. Where are the powerful results for Maria? What are You doing?*

So far, the only results their prayers had yielded in Maria's life were more behavior problems and a suicide attempt. Andrew tried not to let himself feel discouraged. *God is still in control,* he reminded himself.

It wasn't long, however, before more bad news arrived.

"Andrew, get in here!" Erik called. "You've got to see this! You're on TV! Hurry!"

Andrew ran into the other room and sat down on a chair in front of the television set. He and Erik watched as the news trailer began. The music intensified, and stock footage of convicts in prison flashed across the screen.

"He is a dangerous convict who spent time in prison in the United States for armed robbery and kidnapping," the announcer's voice said, "and now he is hiding in the mountains of Monteverde, Costa Rica! We have the exclusive story tonight, right here on channel 11 just before *Latin American Idol.*"

Andrew and Erik stared at the screen with their jaws hanging open.

"No," Andrew finally groaned, putting his hands in his hair and tilting his face toward the ceiling. "Oh, no. What have we done?"

Erik switched off the television and turned to face Andrew. "I hate to mention this, but *Latin American Idol* is one of the most watched programs on television in Costa Rica. The whole country will be tuned in to watch."

"The whole *country?*" Andrew repeated. "This is a nightmare. They completely missed the point of how God has changed my life, and they're capitalizing on the fact that I'm a felon. My idea is backfiring. On national television."

"Maybe it won't be that bad," Erik suggested.

"Not that bad?" Andrew said. "Most of our school kids' parents watch that show! What are they going to say when they find out the person who teaches their kids' Bible and English classes is a 'dangerous convict from the United States who spent time in prison for armed robbery and kidnapping'?"

Erik sank down in the chair next to him. "It's out of our hands now," he said quietly. "We'll just have to pray, wait, and hope for the best."

The same news trailer appeared again and again throughout the day. Andrew felt sick every time he heard the intense music blasting from a television set.

God, all I ever meant to do was bring You glory, and now look what I've done, Andrew prayed. *You know my intentions were good. Please turn this bad situation into something positive.*

The day dragged on. Andrew tried to keep himself occupied by teaching his classes and grading papers, but the distraction of the looming television feature kept interrupting his thoughts. After dinner Andrew and Erik sat down in front of the television set.

"Here goes," Erik said. He pushed the button, and the screen came to life.

The broadcast began with two women talking back and forth and laughing together. *Come on, come on, just get to it,* Andrew thought.

Finally the woman in the red dress turned her attention to the next story. "He was in prison in the United States for kidnapping and armed robbery," she began.

The woman in the black dress chimed in. "Now he is hiding in the mountains of Monteverde."

"Reporter Jose Miguel Cruz found him and brings us the story," the woman in the red dress concluded.

The intense music blasted from the television set again, and Andrew watched with dread as stock footage of police in a high-speed chase appeared. The small white car they were chasing crashed, and police pulled a man from the car and arrested him.

That's not even how it happened, Andrew lamented to himself.

"He was arrested for seven kidnappings and armed robberies," Jose Miguel Cruz said, as footage of a prison cafeteria appeared. "A dangerous youth from the United States. Now he is hiding in the mountains of Monteverde, Costa Rica."

Footage of prisoners fighting in a recreation yard in prison appeared.

Andrew shook his head and sighed. "This is not happening," he whispered.

Jose Miguel Cruz continued. "And this is how we found him."

Suddenly, the image switched to actual footage of Andrew singing "Jesus Loves Me" with his class. Andrew sat up in his chair.

The reporter briefly explained how Andrew had been arrested at the age of 16 and placed in prison. They showed a clip of Andrew talking about how he'd initially been told he would be in prison for life.

"But," the reporter continued, "he found hope in a special Book."

Andrew breathed a sigh of relief as they showed the film of him explaining how his mom had sent a Bible to him in prison, and how he'd found hope in the stories of God helping people through their problems. The image cut to Andrew walking through the village carrying his Bible.

"After 10 years in prison," the reporter said, "he was freed by clemency from the governor of Washington State. He was set free in 2005 and is now 30 years old. He is traveling around the world giving his testimony to motivate others."

"Look!" Erik laughed, pointing at the screen. "There you are in the classroom with the kids!"

"Actually, he is working in Costa Rica as a volunteer missionary teacher. At this school he teaches Bible classes from the same Book that changed his life," the reporter said.

Andrew appeared on the screen again, this time speaking in Spanish. "This life is not fair. It is difficult at times, and there are many problems. But God can help us through them. He has given us reason to hope."

"There you are too!" Andrew laughed when Erik appeared.

"We would like to have the opportunity to visit prisons and jails here in the country in order to share this message of hope with prisoners that have no hope," Erik explained in the footage. "Andrew can use his testimony and commitment to service to motivate them. And when they leave prison, they can experience this same happiness and freedom found in the Bible."

As more pictures of Andrew teaching in his classroom appeared, the reporter ended his segment with a final announcement: "Andrew will be volunteering here for the remainder of the year. Many people around the world have already heard his testimony."

After a brief scene showing Andrew singing with his school kids, the screen switched back to the two female anchors.

"That was awesome!" Erik said. "And we thought it was—"

"Wait, wait," Andrew said. "The women are still talking."

Andrew and Erik leaned in to listen.

"His testimony brings something beautiful to my mind. There are a lot of people who wonder, 'How is it possible for people like him to be a new person?'" The woman in the red dress said. "Well, it is because God, Jesus, entered his life, and God uses imperfect people to show His own perfection."

Andrew was stunned as he listened.

"And look at the power of God's Word!" the woman in the black dress added. "I am a believer—I admit it—and I know that Carolina is a believer as well. If there are nonbelievers who are listening, we would like to apologize to them. But we are addressing those who believe and are strengthening their faith. Look at the power of God's Word! His mom didn't go and nag him, nor did she say anything to him. She just gave him a Bible, and through reading the Word of the Lord, which is the living Word, he experienced a radical change, which can be brought about only by the Lord. It was so radical and final as well. Wow, what a wonderful story!"

Andrew and Erik sat in front of the television with their mouths open. Most of the country of Costa Rica had just tuned in to hear about God's transforming power not only from Andrew and Erik but from the two women who hosted the program as well.

"Incredible," Erik said.

"Amazing," Andrew added. "More than we could have asked for. And that's how God takes care of business."

The next morning Andrew awoke at 4:30 a.m. Although sunrise was still an hour away, the edges of the sky were beginning to blush with pink-ish-orange light. The birds were already awake, and the trees were alive with the sound of their morning songs as Andrew walked down the path to the classroom.

Erik was already there. They chatted for a few minutes, and then began their prayer time together. They took turns thanking God for the amazing testimony they'd been able to share on national television. Then they placed each of their students' names on the prayer altar before God, asking for the Spirit to move in their hearts and create the kind of hunger that can only be satisfied by God's presence.

"And now, God, we desperately lift Maria up to You. We know she is Your daughter and You love her. We know that it is Your desire for her to know You and have the kind of peace that comes from You—the kind of peace that will soothe the pain and anger that is trying to destroy her," Andrew prayed. "God, I know that if she could only experience You the way I have, she would love You too."

While he was praying, there was a noise at the door, and Andrew stopped talking and looked up.

"What is it?" Erik asked, opening his eyes.

"Look," Andrew whispered.

Maria stood in the doorway, her hands clasped together as she looked at them. Her hair was clean and pulled out of her eyes. She tucked a strand behind her ear as she looked at them and smiled shyly.

When she finally spoke, it sounded like one long sentence with no pauses. "*Profe,*" she said to Andrew, "I want to be healthy—I don't want to eat white rice anymore. I want to eat brown rice because it is better for me, and I want to eat vegetables and fruits and stop eating soda and candy. Also, I have never exercised, but I see you guys running, and I want to exercise too, so I can be healthy. Also, I have started to read the Bible, and I want to read the whole thing. I've never read it before. I want to be different, *Profe*. Can you help me?"

Andrew looked at Erik, and then back at Maria. He couldn't believe his ears. When the shock finally wore off a little, he smiled at Maria and nodded.

God, You are amazing, Andrew breathed. *You're making all things new. Just as You promised.*

As the steamy Costa Rican jungle welcomed a new sunrise, Andrew stepped out of his classroom into the morning light. He shielded his eyes and looked at the horizon where the mountains met the sky. His time in Costa Rica would end in a few short weeks. He didn't know where he would go next or what kind of challenges awaited him in his next adventure, but God knew. And that's all Andrew needed to know.

Epilogue

Later, at Cedar Creek Corrections Center . . .

Pat sat down at the computer, fingers poised above the keyboard. His cellie, Junior, had gotten another letter from Andy and shared it with everyone. This time it was from Costa Rica. Andy had been sending pictures from all over—Mexico, Venezuela, Thailand, Costa Rica. And every time the letters arrived with the stories about the kids in the orphanages and the school where Andy taught, it made these tough guys in prison want to cry.

Andy, "The Kid"—one of them, somebody who had showered in the grimy showers, slept in the same cells, ate the same mystery food at meal time, took the same classes, and experienced the same prison system—was actually on the outside doing good in all those places. Living a life Pat and the other guys could only imagine as they sat inside the walls of the prison.

Pat enjoyed the letters and pictures so much he decided to write to Andy himself, and there he sat by the computer, fingers suspended above the keyboard as he tried to figure out what to say.

"Hey, what are you doing?" one of the other guys asked.

"Remember that kid, Andy, who sent us pictures?" Pat said. "Well, I'm typing a letter to him."

The other guy leaned over to look at the pictures. "H'mmm," he said. "That's interesting, because there's a flyer over on the door with a picture of a guy who's a missionary from around the world who's going to be speaking here tonight. And it looks a lot like the guy you're talking about."

Pat jumped up and ran over to the door to look at the flyer. When he looked at the picture, his mouth dropped open. It couldn't be . . . but it was. "That's him!" he said. "That's Andy!"

Fifteen minutes later Andrew walked in. The guys found out he'd gotten permission to come speak at Cedar Creek Corrections Center, and had arrived there before Pat had gotten the chance to type a single word of his letter.

That night Pat, Junior, and the rest of the guys came to the chapel to hear Andrew speak. Andrew told them his story of finding God, his clemency, and how he had come to be a missionary.

"You know, it took me a while to see it, but if I hadn't failed at UW," Andrew said, "I might have missed out on my greatest calling. Now I'm seeing God work in peoples' lives all over the world. Sometimes what we see as failures are God's opportunities in disguise."

They heard more stories of Andrew's mission adventures, including a story about a girl named Maria who gave her heart to God. She had been angry and in trouble and had even tried to commit suicide at one point, but Andrew and his friend had prayed for her consistently, and she had eventually given her heart to God. After that, she was a completely different person—a model student and an example to the other kids. Andrew said he couldn't believe the change in her.

The guys felt ecstatic to be able to talk to Andrew and ask him questions. He had just returned from teaching in Costa Rica for six months, and he told them that within a few days of his return he'd received three separate invitations from three completely unrelated people telling him they needed him in Thailand, and asking him if he'd come back. He said he knew with absolute certainty that God was calling him back there, and he was flying out in a few days. He promised more letters and more pictures.

"After all these years of taking classes, reading the Bible, traveling the world, and exploring other cultures," Andrew said, "all I know is that I need Jesus Christ. Every day."

Before Andrew left, he told them that he believed God had a plan for each of the guys there—God was working in their lives, too. They just had to be open to it.

That night when Andy said goodbye to everyone and walked out of Cedar Creek Corrections Center, he left something behind for Pat, Junior, and all of the other prisoners to share.

Hope.